"When I was at school, I wanted to study geography be
the world, but the geographical knowledge, which I wa
within me a sense of alienation and feelings of being o
scholars – a colonized object to be studied. As a black s
to be an explorer or a researcher. This brilliant book removes the curiosity of geographers from its racist foundations and opens up new and inclusive ways of seeing and knowing the world."

Professor Patricia Daley, *Professor of the Human Geography of Africa, University of Oxford*

"Taking inspiration from postcolonial theory, Black studies, critical geography and beyond, Puttick poses the everyday and the local as sites and concepts with the potential to reanimate geography teaching and revivify children's geographical imaginations. In the wake of the decolonial turn, this engagingly written, fascinating and thoroughly compelling book is an essential read for geography teachers, teacher trainers or indeed anyone involved in geography education research. A vital contribution."

Professor Tariq Jazeel, *Professor of Human Geography, University College London*

"This book undoubtedly weaves together significant ideas and stories, in insightful and thoughtful ways, for geography education. Though, the real joy of reading *The Geography Teaching Adventure* is the space it opens up for the reader to actively participate in enriching conversations about the imperatives and possibilities for reclaiming exploration. The book serves as a potent reminder of why the often invisible intellectual endeavours of teachers are so vital to sustaining the ways in which geography as a subject evolves, across time and space, as it is brought to life in classrooms with and for children and young people."

Grace Healy, *Education Director (Secondary) at the David Ross Education Trust*

"An inspirational call to action for a new way of seeing the world and learning and teaching in Geography – how to help change one of the subjects often seen by children as being boring at school to become the most interesting."

Professor Danny Dorling, *Halford Mackinder Professor of Human Geography, University of Oxford*

The Geography Teaching Adventure

Children are born explorers, full of wonder and hungry for stories about the world. What role might geography teaching play? What geographical stories do we tell about the world? What stories do we tell about geography itself? The book revisits an older vision of geography that is much bigger than exams and memorising information: dreams of adventure and discovery. But where geography's imperial past used these tools for domination and control, this book reclaims exploration to nurture wonder and tell better stories that work towards more just, equitable and sustainable futures.

Positioning geography teaching in relation to major global challenges, author Steve Puttick argues that the subject has a unique role to play through its ability to think across natural and social sciences in equipping young people with the skills and knowledge they need to respond. The book offers a critical and accessible analysis of geography's entanglements with colonialism by exploring the striations of Empire in the subject. Each chapter draws on a wide range of research in geography, and finishes with practical activities and questions for reflection that can be used individually and collectively to support teachers' ongoing professional development.

The book is essential reading for all geography teachers at any stage of their career, as well as geography teacher educators, subject leads and school leaders with responsibility for curriculum development.

Steve Puttick is Associate Professor of Teacher Education. He is a curriculum tutor for the Geography PGCE and MSc Learning and Teaching and fellow of St Anne's College at the University of Oxford, UK.

The Geography Teaching Adventure

Reclaiming Exploration to Inspire Curriculum and Pedagogy

Steve Puttick

LONDON AND NEW YORK

Designed cover image: © Immersive Trails

First published 2024
by Routledge
4 Park Square, Milton Park, Abingdon, Oxon OX14 4RN

and by Routledge
605 Third Avenue, New York, NY 10158

Routledge is an imprint of the Taylor & Francis Group, an informa business

© 2024 Steve Puttick

The right of Steve Puttick to be identified as author of this work has been asserted in accordance with sections 77 and 78 of the Copyright, Designs and Patents Act 1988.

All rights reserved. No part of this book may be reprinted or reproduced or utilised in any form or by any electronic, mechanical, or other means, now known or hereafter invented, including photocopying and recording, or in any information storage or retrieval system, without permission in writing from the publishers.

Trademark notice: Product or corporate names may be trademarks or registered trademarks, and are used only for identification and explanation without intent to infringe.

British Library Cataloguing-in-Publication Data
A catalogue record for this book is available from the British Library

ISBN: 978-1-032-34356-3 (hbk)
ISBN: 978-1-032-34357-0 (pbk)
ISBN: 978-1-003-32168-2 (ebk)

DOI: 10.4324/9781003321682

Typeset in Melior
by codeMantra

Contents

1	**The adventure**	**1**
	Introduction	1
	Children's geographies and everyday experiences	4
	Practical theorising	6
	Conclusion	9
	Questions and activities	10
	Notes	10
	References	11
2	**Exploration and geography**	**13**
	Introduction	13
	Origin stories and Vasco Da Gama	14
	Joseph Conrad	19
	Exploration by warfare	23
	Conclusions	26
	Questions and activities	26
	Notes	27
	References	28
3	**Striations of Empire in school geography**	**29**
	Introduction	29
	School geography 'making a world of difference'	31
	Racist geographies of Empire	34
	Geography and Eurocentrism	39
	Defending the Empire	40
	Conclusions	49
	Questions and activities	50
	Notes	50
	References	51
4	**Power, knowledge and prisoners**	**53**
	Introduction	53
	Conclusions	70
	Questions and activities	71
	Notes	71
	References	72

5 Journeys of information **74**
Introduction 74
Mountains, information and hidden people 76
Online journeys of information 79
New journeys of information, old stories about statistics 83
Conclusions 87
Questions and activities 88
Notes 89
References 90

6 Where should we start from? **92**
Introduction 92
Starting from Europe 93
Starting with al-Idrisi 95
Starting from the Global South 98
Starting from the local and everyday 99
Conclusions 109
Questions and activities 110
Notes 111
References 112

7 What stories should we tell? **114**
Introduction 114
Plots 118
Characters 120
Conflict 123
Here's to the storytellers 124
Questions and activities 125
Notes 126
References 127

Index 129

1 The adventure

Introduction

Children are born explorers, full of wonder and hungry for stories about the world. What role might geography teaching play? What geographical stories do we tell about the world? What stories do we tell about geography itself? What kinds of stories could we be telling? This introductory chapter sets the book within the broader context of teaching geography, sketching some of the stories that have been told about the purpose of geography in education. It concludes by discussing the idea of 'practical theorising', conceptualising teaching as an amazing, challenging, complex and exciting endeavour that demands teachers be *geographers* in education. The introductory chapter also introduces some of the key terms which help to shape the broad framing of the debates the book engages with. Putting some of these concepts to use, Chapter 2 offers a brief history of adventure and geography. Adventure has played a formative role in geography, and this chapter highlights the deep entanglements between geographical adventure and racist, extractive colonial projects of empire. I try to reclaim – flipping upside down and inside out – geographical adventure, beginning with a shift in scales. By questioning an obsession with distant, far-flung places, I narrow the scale to foreground the local and everyday as the heart of adventure. Chapter 3 introduces Rex Walford's seminal book *Geography in British Schools 1850–2000: Making a world of difference*. Inspired by Jazeel's metaphor of 'striations of empire', I critically examine the striations of empire that are visible in *Geography in British Schools*. Striations are evidence of powerful forces that have moved over the land, and through this analysis I question the nature of the 'difference' that school geography has made. The themes of racist geographies of empire, geography and Eurocentrism and defending the Empire, all bear witness to the ways in which school geography has been shaped by these powerful forces. Arguments about power are then followed further in Chapter 4 through critiques of the concept of 'powerful knowledge' and the popular book *Prisoners of Geography*. Themes of knowledge and information are developed through the idea of

DOI: 10.4324/9781003321682-1

journeys of information in Chapter 5, which also prompts questions about where the information that is presented in classrooms comes from. The critical work of the early chapters is designed to create space from which a more expansive vision for school geography might be developed. Reclaiming exploration to inspire curriculum and pedagogy begins with the work of unpicking, disentangling and more openly addressing some of the deep striations of Empire that are routed into the geographical tradition and which I show have shaped school geography. Through the final three chapters I sketch a more expansive vision by addressing three big questions about the future of geography teaching: Where should we start from? Where should we go? What stories should we tell? Where past generations launched perilous voyages seeking distant lands in hope of riches, fame and national pride, geographers of today and tomorrow have equally fraught adventures ahead of them. But today's and tomorrow's geographers have more complex challenges to face, and these reclaimed, reimagined adventures are working towards more valuable aims: addressing historic inequalities and their stubbornly enduring legacies, reducing, mitigating and adapting to climate and ecological crises in the hope of more sustainable, equitable and just futures. All of these aims make searches for the source of a river or the intrigue of a blank map seem like a simple 'walk in the park' or a game of hide and seek. The kinds of geographical adventures that you need to equip your students to embark on are the most urgent, important and consequential of any of the journeys that humanity has navigated.

This book is about stories, wonder and exploration. It is about the ways in which geography teaching might reclaim adventure to nurture wonder and tell better stories that work towards more just, equitable and sustainable futures. By revisiting older ideas about adventure and exploration I want to recapture some of the excitement and romance that can be side-lined in formal education systems overshadowed by what Stephen Ball calls the 'terror of performativity'.[1] However, I hope that the book doesn't give the impression of a romanticised view of the past. There were many problems with some previous geographical work that bring shame to the subject. Others have addressed these issues far more extensively than there is space to do here,[2] and a summary is outlined in Chapter 2 of the entanglements between empire, imperialism and geography. These entanglements were and are extremely messy. Racist, colonial domination that at times was directly served and promoted by geography and geographers. Seeking to reclaim adventure, and inspired by a range of other critiques, I hope, in Katherine McKittrick's (2021, p. 187) words, 'to sustain wonder'.[3] My hope through this book is to sketch a vision for teaching geography that sustains wonder and does not settle for simplistic stories about people, places and things.

Wonder is often associated with the widest of scales; sparkling polar expanses, vast oceans, innumerable stars in the sky at night, mass-anythings. This is certainly Joseph Conrad's geography, which he describes discovering for himself as 'the geography of open spaces and wide horizons'. However, this expansive geography was not reflected in his school curriculum. Instead, his experience of school geography was shaped:

> by persons of no romantic sense of the real, ignorant of the great possibilities of active life; with no desire for struggle, no notion of the wide spaces of the world – mere bored professors, in fact, who were not only middle-aged, but looked as if they had never been young. And their geography was very much like themselves, a bloodless thing, with a dry skin covering a repulsive armature of uninteresting bones.[4]

Full of provocative metaphors and imagery, Conrad's geography is about ambition, action and challenge: life with blood coursing through its veins, breathing deeply and fully experiencing the 'wide spaces of the world'. Ideas about scale run throughout this book, and I want us to (mostly) zoom in, moving away from Conrad's distant and wide-open spaces. Scale is fundamental to teaching geography, cutting across all other concepts and topics. Scale has also been an important part of the backdrop against which recent discussions in geography education have taken place. These discussions have centred around a distinction between 'everyday knowledge' and 'powerful knowledge'. In accounts about powerful knowledge, everyday knowledge is restricted to the local, whereas powerful knowledge is objective, looking over and generalising to every- and any-where. I want to put forward an argument against such a dismissal of everyday knowledges that have been associated with popular ideas about 'powerful knowledge'[5]: instead, my argument focuses on the value and wonder that comes through attention to the local and everyday. In part, reclaiming adventure is about the re-enchantment of the everyday and the reimagining of 'other', 'distant' places and peoples as, firstly and most importantly, local and everyday. Shifting scales in this way changes an exotic other to someone else's local and everyday. Inspired by, among others, Jazeel's *Postcolonialism*,[6] McKittrick's *Dear Science and Other Stories*,[7] Yusoff's *A Billion Black Anthropocenes or None*,[8] Said's *Orientalism*,[9] and Chakrabarty's *Provincializing Europe*,[10] I return throughout the book to reconsider how we might tell better stories about our own position in the world and the geographies through which we come to know the world by giving greater attention to the local and everyday. It is not (at least not to begin with) distant, wide-open spaces that I want to encourage us to explore. Instead, my argument is that there is wonder and adventure in the local and everyday, even if it is not quite what we first expected and requires us to question some assumptions and readjust our perspective.

One label I am using to refer to these ideas about reclaiming exploration is through a 'pedagogy of exploration': an approach to teaching geography that prioritises being geographical in ways that draw on and critically engage with geographical traditions. There is a tension here between the ways that exploration prompts associations with an unstructured 'discovery approach', and also with highly structured 'knowledge-led' approaches. For the former, the term 'exploration' evokes ideas of 'discovery'. For the latter, the priority given to disciplinary – geographical – expertise seems to align it with 'knowledge-led' or 'core-knowledge' movements. Both of these broad positions have generated very strong responses from quite different directions. In *reclaiming exploration* I want to revisit the use and development of both discovery and geographical knowledge in teaching geography. One aspect of the disposition towards adventure that I am arguing for is about the whole atmosphere of geography education being one in which exploration saturates and inspires everything. Central to this is telling better stories about the world and about geography itself, and doing so in ways that empower young people to understand and shape their own geographies.

Reimagining the everyday as potential sites of adventure, and reconsidering geography itself – giving attention to the 'geographies of geography'[11] – means that even the textbook on your students' desk might become a source of adventure. Ideas, concepts and the stories we tell with and about them are central to exploration. Maybe this involves some uncomfortable critiquing of populism, national exceptionalism, the othering of countries, regions, peoples and neighbours, neoliberalism, extractive and exploitative practices and challenging lifestyles that rely on global inequalities and exacerbate the unequal risks associated with anthropogenic climate change.

I hope this book will be useful for both those at the start of their teaching careers (in whatever kind of formal or informal setting you find yourself) and those with more years already served. I also hope that it might contribute to ongoing discussions around geography education research, including the relationships between geography as an academic discipline and a school subject. To serve these potentially different interests, I have made use of practical sections at the end of each chapter to apply the arguments to the contexts of schools and other settings where geography is taught. These application sections include questions for discussion, practical strategies and insights into practice that I hope might be of interest for teachers, departments and in Initial Teacher Education (ITE) and Continuing Professional Development (CPD). I have also made use of footnotes as a way of providing some additional detail, commentary and references for those who would like to follow the debates a little further than I have space for in the main body of the text.

Children's geographies and everyday experiences

I began this chapter by claiming that 'children are born explorers, full of wonder and hungry for stories about the world'. The sub-discipline of children's geographies often sheds light on these points often by trying to understand how children themselves describe and perceive the world around them and their relationship to it (Hammond et al., 2022). Some of this research focuses on children's experiences of education and their perceptions of geography. For example, Hopwood (2009) looks in detail at the complexity of how secondary school students conceive of geography. His open and flexible methodology involved using ethnographic methods to spend time with students during their geography lessons, and through this he generated detailed understandings of students' learning and conceptions of geography. He concludes that their ideas about geography are not fixed or simple. Instead, he finds them to often be 'loose collections of context-dependent ideas rather than coherent or unified views' (p. 185). Across these students' understandings of geography there is a strong sense of different areas of the subject, mainly framed as human and physical, which the students see as being associated with detail, facts and explanation (physical), and affect and opinions (human). One student – named through the pseudonym Sara – described geography as being the study of people and places, and Hopwood emphasises the idea of spatial variation as being central to Sara's views about geography. For example, in discussing differences between cultures in different countries and the ways in which, through geography, students might learn about these cultures that are 'different from your own'. These differences are presented in stark terms: in 'other parts of the world, the way people live…it's somewhere else and they think completely different to what we do"' (p. 192). *Completely different.*

Another contrast that comes out of the literature on children's perceptions of the world is between 'natural' and 'man made' environments. For example, Walshe's (2021) eco-capabilities work provides striking examples of the distinctiveness – the difference – that children (and also the artists, teachers and researchers) felt between the time they spent 'in nature' on the project and the rest of their 'normal lives'. There are widely held beliefs about modern disconnection from nature, with increases in screen time and heightened perceptions of risk and danger outside cited as reasons for decreases in our connections with nature. Who counts as part of 'our' leads us to question the ways in which this is differentially felt and experienced across racialised, gendered and classed dimensions. Huth's (2013) *The Lost Art of Finding Our Way* opens by posing a question comparing the knowledge of a modern commuter against that of a fisherman who lived 3,000 years ago. The discussion focuses on how much information they both have, and where this information comes from. For the modern commuter, Huth suggests that their information comes primarily from the smartphone, whereas the fisherman's information is embodied. He judges the modern commuter a little harshly, concluding that 'while the device-addicted commuter may seem oblivious to and clueless about his surroundings, his ancestors proved that humans *can* absorb exceedingly subtle environmental clues to find their way' (p. 2). In the story, the fisherman's intimate, confident knowledge of the weather is contrasted against the commuter's to paint a picture that is similar to Hitching's (2010) research on seasonal climate change and professional office workers. After a cold night in London, Hitchings describes the morning routine of a lawyer commuting from their home to their office in the city three miles to the south. Overnight, the air settling over London had changed. Making its journey from the polar north, the temperature had dropped, and the cold air left a frost decorating the pavements and other surfaces. Below zero: a change in the state of H_2O from a liquid to a solid. Newly laid low-friction layers cover city walkways. Yet these changes are not immediately felt by the commuter who we imagine emerging from an insulated flat with double-glazed windows and central heating. Their busy-ness with business insulates them both literally and symbolically from the changes in the weather that happened while they slept: the lawyer

> already had to deal with the expectation that he would present himself in certain ways at work and this limited the extent to which he could respond through his clothing...he was also initially oblivious to this seasonal cold snap because he was following his usual morning pattern.
>
> (p. 282)

The morning routine (what Hitchings describes as being 'on autopilot') initially in a space insulated from the climate in which he is ironing a shirt, getting breakfast and then going downstairs and walking to the Tube station is punctuated by the change in surface and the interaction between leather-soled brogues and ice-coated tarmac. 'Only then did he realise how his standard system of dealing with this brief spell of outdoor experience was insufficiently robust to handle the legacy of the night before' (p. 282). Was the commuter a geographer? What might you hope your geography teaching would do to transform and reimagine their morning routine? One of the activities at the end of this chapter is inspired by this commuter and questions about how geography teaching might contribute to changing their relationship with the environment, stimulating discussion about the aims and purposes of the subject through a (frost-covered) concrete example.

The argument running through this chapter and across the book is that teaching geography holds the potential to enable us to reimagine our relationship with the world. Transforming a morning commute into an adventure through the re-enchantment of the everyday. Maybe this means that we become more well-informed, more curious and more aware. Maybe we ask more questions, or maybe it's not about *more* but about our engagement with the world being deeper and richer. Knowing, being, living and breathing that involves an active switching away from auto-pilot. This kind of exploration is holistic: it is not only about the knowledge of the weather and the city, nor it is only about the experience of the weather and the city. It is about embodied, physical, material, emotional experiences which at the same time are conceptual and theoretical. The idea of practical theorising offers one way to understand the relationships between the practical and theoretical in the context of teaching.

Practical theorising

Teacher education continues to wrestle with questions about the relationship between the practical and the theoretical. At times the descriptions of these relationships can be polemical with practical and theoretical being pitted against each other. A populist version of this argument was made by the then Education

Secretary Michael Gove who wrote in the Daily Mail that he 'refused to surrender to the Marxist teachers hell-bent on destroying our schools'.[12] In his account, 'theory' (particularly Marxist theory) and people producing theory (particularly university-based academics, but also 'Marxist teachers') are bad, and are contrasted against others who are purely practical (being without 'political motivation'). Gove's later infamous update of this argument – this time as Lord Chancellor during Britain's referendum of membership of the European Union – saw him claiming the country had 'had enough of experts'. Theory is characterised as being out of touch with the practical reality that everyday people have to deal with. Practical theorising challenges and rejects these caricatures by re-framing the relationships between practice and theory to present a deeply connected, interactive approach to teaching. Practical theorising describe how teachers might develop through critically and intelligently engaging with multiple types of evidence which I am extending here to offers as a model of engaging with the academic discipline of geography. Through the idea of practical theorising, teachers are positioned in an exciting and challenging space interweaving pedagogical and disciplinary knowledges. The vision of practical theorising is ambitious and highly respectful of the teacher's knowledge and skill. In this model, teaching is a dynamic, complex activity and it is not possible to simply tell teachers how to teach. It is not possible to prescribe exactly what to teach. In part, this is because of the uniqueness of each individual, class, relationship and situation: the same content will not result in the same lesson or exactly the same learning every time it is taught. In part, this is also because of the nature of subjects themselves. Geographical knowledge is (at least in part) illusive, shifting, dynamic and contested. It can't just be transmitted; it needs to be explored. Getting into the subject knowledge of geography is an adventure.

Practical theorising has been at the heart of Oxford's initial teacher education work (with the model of the course being referred to as the Oxford Internship Scheme), and so some of the discussion around it references specific challenges and opportunities of that model and context. The ideal of practical theorising places a high degree of value on teachers' agency, intellectual freedom and potential to thoughtfully and critically engage with, recontextualise and experiment with an expansive range of evidence. Critiques have focused on the (undue?) burden that this freedom places on beginning teachers: would it not be easier (and fairer?) to simply tell them what to do? Giving all beginning teachers a simple list of practices they need to learn and do would generate standardisation of practice and alleviate beginning teachers of the hard work of making decisions about what to do in the complex range of situations they face? As Burn, Mutton, and Thompson (2023) put it: why persist with practical theorising when it's so much easier in theory than in practice? This challenge is also unavoidable in this book's conception of geography teaching as an adventure that has a high view of teachers and teaching. Practical theorising sees one aspect of teaching as an act of translation. In the geographical contexts, we might think about the ways in which teachers translate landscapes, processes, concepts and places. Making the infinitely complex understandable, manageable and knowable. Maybe a desire for adventure also involves embracing a sense of immensity and complexity that cannot be easily translated. In Jazeel's (2019) terms, we might embrace 'untranslatability. Moments of untranslatability are in fact immensely productive encounters with incommensurability' (p. 215). Underpinning the conception of practical theorising for teacher education is a belief in the complexity of teaching which finds strong resonances here with Jazeel's call for embracing untranslatability. Reality – even the mundane everyday – is so incredible, so breath-taking, so awe-inspiring, complex and counterintuitive that it escapes our simple categorisations and explanations. The teacher beings a description "This town is..." and before *is* passes our lips, *this town* escapes. To mix metaphors, the reality runs away through our fingers like water as we try to close our grip on it. In Castree's (2005) terms: 'The nature that geographers study (in all senses of the term) is not, [he argues,] to be confused with the things the term describes.' Instead, nature is 'a concept or idea, not the real world of species, landforms and bodies...[we must not] treat this knowledge as a 'mirror' held up to the natural world...' (pp. 42–43). Just as in practical theorising teachers cannot be given a simple list of 'how to teach', here there is a call for recognising the epistemic limits of theories and models, giving attention to and helping students to come to realise the important senses in which spaces, places and people '*cannot* be known through these typologies and categorizations' (Jazeel, 2019, pp. 215–216). The idea of 'epistemic limits' is about recognising that knowledge is produced and positioned in distinctive ways that bring certain implications. Knowledge is not an object, but instead is social, relational and transitory. Decolonial and postcolonial critiques of geographical knowledge have highlighted a tension between seeing knowledge in this way – as something less powerful and certain than it might be assumed to be – but also in recognising some knowledges as being hugely powerful. In Heyman's (2000, p. 301) account, the point is to 'deobjectify' knowledge, exposing 'the classroom as a site of practical political engagement and disrupts the boundary between theory and praxis'. Using explicitly social terms, Heyman describes classrooms as a coming together for making meaning and knowledge about places that we live in:

> Knowledge is not merely an object to be used as an instrument of technocratic rationality with which to better manage the world. Rather, it is itself a dynamic pedagogical encounter. Viewed this way, it has the potential to empower rather than dominate.
>
> (p. 301)

In the context of academic geography, knowledge can – Heyman argues – still be treated instrumentally, that is, as something that can be disseminated and circulated unproblematically. Think of a polished, well-presented PDF report listing five takeaway points in its executive summary, and about how this representation of the knowledge represents it as an object that hides the messy tracked changes

Word document with its scored-through, underlined, highlighted, commented-on text in progress, which in turn fails to represent fully the thoughts, emotions, conflicts and partialities of the authors, who in turn fail to see, hear, measure, smell, feel and analyse fully the living, breathing, moving world of their study. 'Deobjectifying knowledge' is partly about peeling back these layers to challenge its status 'as a commodity that can be readily exchanged for the price of a book, a consulting fee, or university tuition' (p. 299). Against this commodification, Heyman argues that 'the work of knowledge production does *not* end with a written text' (p. 299). One pedagogical implication, which presents a massive challenge and seems counterintuitive to huge swathes of the literature on 'how to teach', is presented by Heyman as a challenge to develop 'more sophisticated approaches to pedagogy that do not reduce knowledge to information that is easily transmissible' (p. 299). This kind of teaching – the geography teaching adventure – is about:

> accepting the dynamic, interactive, and political nature of the pedagogical encounter mean defining the classroom as a vital public space that needs to be defended against the forces of commoditization that would reduce it to a mere medium of transmission. A radical pedagogy that resists the closure of knowledge also resists the clientization of students.
>
> (p. 301)

Or maybe the perspective that I am arguing for is about more than 'accepting' this, and instead is about embracing, enjoying and wrestling with the dynamic, interactive and unavoidably political nature of the pedagogical encounter. The stories that have been told about the world and about geography are neither neutral nor apolitical. Reclaiming exploration is partly about retelling these stories.

Conclusion

This chapter has sketched some of the big themes in this book on the geography teaching adventure, including: children's sense of wonder and exploration; the complexity, challenge and opportunity of teaching as conceived of through practical theorising; and sustaining wonder. The geography teaching adventure seeks to rediscover and reimagine some of the brilliance and excitement that is evoked through the ways in which geographers have generated new understandings of the world and our relation to it. The *re*discovering and *re*imagining parts of this are about critically evaluating geography's messy entanglements with empire and extractive colonial agendas. These entanglements are examined through a metaphor of *striations of empire* in Chapter 3, after discussing further geographers' engagements with exploration and adventure in Chapter 2. Each chapter in the book finishes with suggested 'questions and activities' which hopefully raise some useful points for further discussion, implications for practice and activities for individuals and groups to critically reflect on.

Questions and activities

Adventure. What does this word mean to you? What ideas, images and feelings come to mind when you hear it? To what extent do you think geography teaching should be an adventure? In what ways do you think 'adventure' is not appropriate for thinking about geography teaching? What challenges might you face in seeking to teach geography in ways that embrace and are inspired by ideas about adventure?

In Hitching's description of a lawyer commuting into London, he emphasises the separation between their normal routine on auto-pilot and the change in weather that they go on to encounter. You might like to remind yourself of his account above (and if you have more time available, follow up with the full paper). I wonder what geography this commuter had studied? And how does their geographical understanding relate to the ways in which they anticipate, experience and respond to the changing climatic conditions in which they live, commute and work? Think about this from the perspective of your own geography teaching and the aims towards which you hope it might work. How might your geography teaching transform their morning routine? What knowledge and skills might it equip them with to reimagine their commute?

In the discussion about 'deobjectifying knowledge', I quoted Heyman's critique of a 'closure' of knowledge. Following this metaphor further, what might it mean to 'open' knowledge to students? What examples do you have of knowledge being represented as an 'object' in school geography? What might the implications of these representations be? And in what ways might it be 'deobjectified'?

Notes

1 Ball (2003) describes performativity as 'a technology, a culture and a mode of regulation that employs judgements, comparisons and displays as means of incentive, control, attrition and change – based on rewards and sanctions (both material and symbolic)' (p. 216).
2 For example, see: Kearns (2009, 2021), Hamilton (2020), Norcup (2015), and Esson (2020).
3 These ideas find echoes in West's (2009) calls for a 'bestowal of dignity, grandeur and tragedy on the ordinary lives of everyday people; and an experimental form of life that highlights curiosity, wonder, contingency, adventure, danger, and most importantly, improvisation' (p. xi).
4 Conrad (1924), and for further discussion also see Driver (1992).
5 In particular, through Young's (2013) dichotomy between 'everyday' and 'powerful' knowledge, which follows a longer line of thought in his work. For example, over 20 years ago, reacting to 'post-colonialism', 'feminism' and 'postmodernism' he warned of 'the dangers of invoking experience against the knowledge claims of expertise, science or other bodies of specialist knowledge' (2000, p. 530).
6 Jazeel (2019).
7 McKittrick (2021).

8 Yusoff (2018).
9 Said (1978).
10 Chakrabarty (2000).
11 For example, see Livingstone's (2019) attention to the 'geography of geography', and through the case of climate change, see Mahony and Hulme's (2018) discussion of 'epistemic geographies'; geographies about knowledge and its production and circulation
12 https://www.dailymail.co.uk/debate/article-2298146/I-refuse-surrender-Marxist-teachers-hell-bent-destroying-schools-Education-Secretary-berates-new-enemies-promise-opposing-plans.html

References

Ball, S. J. (2003). The teachers soul and the terrors of performativity. *Journal of Education Policy, 18*, 215–228.

Burn, K., Mutton, T., & Thompson, I. (Eds.). (2023). *Practical Theorising in Teacher Education: Holding Theory and Practice Together*. London: Routledge.

Castree, N. (2005). *Nature*. New York: Routledge.

Chakrabarty, D. (2000). *Provincializing Europe*. Oxford: Princeton University Press.

Conrad, J. (1924). Geography and some explorers. *National Geographic*.

Driver, F. (1992). Geography's empire: Histories of geographical knowledge. *Environment and Planning D: Society and Space, 10*(1), 23–40.

Esson, J. (2020). "The why and the white": Racism and curriculum reform in British geography. *Area, 52*, 708–715. doi:10.1111/area.12475

Hamilton, A. R. (2020). The white unseen: On white supremacy and dangerous entanglements in geography. *Dialogues in Human Geography, 10*(3), 299–303. doi:10.1177/2043820620966489

Hammond, L., Biddulph, M., Catling, S., & McKendrick, J. H. (Eds.). (2022). *Children, Education and Geography: Rethinking Intersections*. London: Routledge.

Heyman, R. (2000). Research, pedagogy, and instrumental geography. *Antipode, 32*(3), 292–307. doi:10.1111/1467-8330.00136

Hitchings, R. (2010). Seasonal climate change and the indoor city worker. *Transaction of the Institute of British Geographers, 35*, 282–298.

Hopwood, N. (2009). UK high school pupils' conceptions of geography: research findings and methodological implications. *International Research in Geographical and Environmental Education*, 18(3), 185–197.

Huth, J. E. (2013). *The Lost Art of Finding Our Way*. London: The Belknap Press of Harvard University Press.

Jazeel, T. (2019). *Postcolonialism*. Abingdon: Routledge.

Kearns, G. (2009). *Geopolitics and Empire: The Legacy of Halford Mackinder*. Oxford: Oxford University Press.

Kearns, G. (2021). Topple the racists 2: Decolonising the space and the institutional memory of geography. *Geography, 106*(1), 4–15. doi:10.1080/00167487.2020.1862575

Livingstone, D. N. (2019). The geographical tradition and the challenges of geography geographised. *Transactions of the Institute of British Geographers, 44*(3), 458–462. doi:10.1111/tran.12299

Mahony, M., & Hulme, M. (2018). Epistemic geographies of climate change: Science, space and politics. *Progress in Human Geography, 42*(3), 395–424. doi:10.1177/0309132516681485

McKittrick, K. (2021). *Dear Science and Other Stories*. Durham: Duke University Press.

Norcup, J. (2015). *Awkward geographies? An historical and cultural geography of the journal Contemporary Issues in Geography and Education (CIGE) (1983–1991).* (PhD). University of Glasgow.

Said, E. (1978). *Orientalism*. London: Penguin.

Walshe, N. (2021). *"It Was Like I Was Not a Person, It Was Like I Was the Nature": Exploring Children's Perceptions of Nature and Wellbeing Through Eco-Capabilities*. Paper presented at the Qual Hub, University of Oxford, Department of Education.

West, C. (2009). *Keeping Faith*. Abingdon: Routledge.

Young, M. (2013). Powerful knowledge: an analytically useful concept or just a 'sexy sounding term'? A response to John Beck's 'Powerful knowledge, esoteric knowledge, curriculum knowledge'. *Cambridge Journal of Education, 43*(2), 195–198.

Young, M. F. D. (2000). Rescuing the Sociology of Educational Knowledge from the Extremes of Voice Discourse: Towards a new theoretical basis for the sociology of the curriculum. *British Journal of Sociology of Education, 21*(4), 523–536. doi:10.1080/713655366

Yusoff, K. (2018). *A Billion Black Anthropocenes or None*. Minneapolis: University of Minnesota Press.

2 Exploration and geography

Introduction

Stories about geography's origins often start by retelling some classic colonial adventures about European pioneers who bravely struck out towards a distant unknown, unlikely ever to return to their homeland. These stories are part of the myth-making of what Chakrabarty calls the 'hyperreal Europe': a fiction of our imagination that is supported by the incredible efforts of these individual men and their achievements in dominating whole swathes of the globe. 'Knowledge is power, geographical knowledge is world-power,'[1] and there are tight connections between these stories about geography and Empire-building power. This disciplinary myth-making traces the true essence of geography's spirit into these men, and so while they were often not strictly doing geographical analysis or explicitly writing the kind of geography that we might immediately recognise as such, their endeavours are claimed to be part of geography's origins. Livingstone's (1992) important account of *The Geographical Tradition* begins with a critical and reflexive discussion of history, narrative and disciplinary myths that explicitly positions all history as being written from certain perspectives and of only ever giving partial accounts. But it then goes on to largely replicate the myths about the individual heroics of these Europeans, praising their skills and determination, and erasing much of the expertise upon which they completely depended.

Almost unconsciously, the construction of geography's disciplinary history is narrowed to European geography and so Livingstone writes that 'The voyaging ventures of the Portuguese are the most natural place to begin'. What do we mean by 'natural?' (Castree, 2005). The naturalness of beginning with Europe is firmly entrenched in the ways that we often tell stories about geography, an idea that is questioned in Chapter 6's discussion *Where should we start from*. To deconstruct some of these adventure narratives in geography, the current chapter critically examines (albeit very briefly and partially) aspects of the history of adventure and geography, thinking through the practice of exploration in geography and the ways in which ideas about adventure and exploration have been defined and used – particularly

DOI: 10.4324/9781003321682-2

in the stories we tell about the beginnings and evolution of the subject. Critically engaging with geography's contribution to the politics and practice of Empire, the chapter introduces some of the key concepts associated with colonial logics of race and extraction and asks how these ideas continue to inform and be reproduced through geography teaching. Through this argument, geography is presented as complex, including both 'shadow and shine': geographical exploration has been tied up with Imperial domination, yet it also offers the tools to undo and reimagine how we might understand, describe and engage with people and places. Teachers have an essential role to play in navigating this complexity as they recontextualise geographical knowledges. But for now, back to the 'natural' start with Portugal and Vasco Da Gama.

Origin stories and Vasco Da Gama

The year is 1487. July. Bartholomeu Dias's small fleet leaves Lisbon, setting out in the hope of being the first to sail from Europe to India. Eight months later they become the first Europeans to sail around the southernmost point of Africa – the Cape of Good Hope – although this was not the name that Dias gave it. Soon after rounding the Cape, and by this time with depleted supplies, exhausted crews, and ships in need of repair, they were faced with storms and forced to turn around. In Livingstone's words, they 'limp[ed] back to Lisbon weather-beaten' (p. 4). Dias named the Cape *Cabo das Tormentas* (Cape of Storms). Later renamed the Cape of Good Hope by Joao II for the hope it offered in making the journey to India possible, the next Portuguese effort ten years later was

> left to the indomitable Vasco Da Gama to go all the way and stake Portugal's claim – now under Manuel I – in India. This he did in 1498 when on 22 May he touched the south-western coast of India, having displayed stunning navigational skills in his route around the Cape and across the Arabian Sea and the Indian Ocean.
>
> (p. 4)

These origin stories – about geography's true essence being found in these brave individuals – are myths. Early accounts of these journeys tell, in many ways, quite different stories about these people, the others on whose knowledge and expertise they depended, and about the kinds of success they achieved. In the case of Vasco Da Gama, journals from the voyages give some insight into the more complex reality of this age of adventure and discovery.

Da Gama's voyage to India began by sailing South, parallel to the Western coast of Africa, and then round the Cape of Good Hope, and North along the Eastern coastline. The journals record a pattern that is repeated as he travels around the coast of Africa. The men get sick, they need food and water and they need information and knowledge, particularly in terms of locational and navigational expertise. Seeking these things, they anchor frequently at various ports along their journey, including; St Helena, Mozambique, Mombasa and Malindi. Each time they go through a process of working out what kind of reception the locals might give them (mainly based on whether the locals are believed to be Moors or Christians). The sailors then take time to heal their sick, stock up on supplies and secure more pilots to navigate and show them the way to their next destination. They also seem obsessed with erecting pillars. Sometimes they ask if the local chief would mind them erecting a pillar, and in other places they just go ahead and do it without asking. These landmarks are not always well received. At the bay of Sam Brás they describe erecting a cross and a pillar, and 'the cross was made out of mizzen-mast, and very high' (Velho, 1500, p. 13).[2] Before they have even left, 'ten or twelve' locals have already come and demolished both the cross and the pillar. Some pillars have lasted longer, or have been rebuilt more recently. The Kenyan port that Da Gama sailed from – Malindi – has a pillar commemorating Da Gama (the Da Gama pillar). A particularly dry review of the pillar on Google maps captures the spirit of it well: "It's a pillar, so don't let your expectations be too high. But the scenery is good." The information board proclaims: "Vasco da Gama and the discovery of the sea route to India". Another poster from the National Museums of Kenya describes the journey:

> One April 7th 1498 the expedition reached Mombasa and on the 13th anchored at Malindi where he established amicable relations with the Sheikh of Malindi, guided by Ahmed Bin Majid, on 20th May 1498 Da Gama reached Calcutta (Calicut – India) after 23 days in the sea.
>
> As a mark of discovery and over-lord ship, he erected a pillar near Sheikh's palace in Malindi town, however its Christian connotation caused discontent among Muslims and was soon taken down. Later under the Portuguese insistence, it was set up at its present location in the 16th Century.

Did you spot the error? Not (only) Da Gama's error of erecting a pillar to mark his 'over-lord ship', but the tourist information's error of Da Gama's arrival port in India of Calcutta. Bracketing the name next to the city – Calcutta (Calicut – India) – is often used to give the current name of the city, updating the British colonial name. However, Calicut and Calcutta are not alternative names for the same place. They refer to two different places over 2,000 km apart. Calicut is now known as Kozhikode and is on the Malabar Coast in the Southern Indian state of Kerala. Calcutta (now Kolkata) is the capital city of West Bengal state. The error of attributing Calicut as Calcutta was repeated more recently in the Independent newspaper in an article on Da Gama.[3] What names are given to places is an important part of these stories about geography and adventure. Just as Da Gama left pillars as a sign of his overlordship, his journals also record their regular practice of designating new names. As they leave ports they often name places and features: departing from Inhambane in southern Mozambique they declare "We called the country *Terra do Boa Gente* (land of good people), and the river *Rio do Cobre* (copper river)" (p. 18), as if the country and river did not already have names.

Just as the practice of naming seems to be the wrong way round (surely the first question is what these places are already called?), so too stories told about a hyper-real Europe often get finances the wrong way round. The riches of the world were not to be found in Europe, but in India, and it was not a case of European wealth and progress bringing civilisation and technological advances to India. The reception of the King of Calicut to Da Gama's gifts offers some insight into the actual nature of this relationship. The gifts that Da Gama brought from Portugal to India are described in his journal as containing: 'four scarlet hoods, six hats, four strings of coral, a case containing six wash-hand basins, a case of sugar, two casks of oil, and two of honey' (p. 60). Gifts which Da Gama asks the King's attendees to deliver to the King:

> They came, and when they saw the present they laughed at it, saying that it was not a thing to offer to a king, that the poorest merchant from Mecca, or any other part of India, gave more, and that if he wanted to make a present it should be in gold, as the king would not accept such things.
>
> (p. 61)

This leads to an embarrassing string of events; the courtiers tell Da Gama to wait for them to come back and take him to the king. Da Gama waits all day, and ends up just left waiting because they don't come back. He thinks about going directly to the King himself, but decides better of it. In the meantime, the Da Gama's crew members are having a great time: 'As to us others, we diverted ourselves, singing and dancing to the sound of trumpets, and enjoyed ourselves much'! The king's attendees then come and get Da Gama the next day, and he is made to wait again; this time for four hours. On entering the King's palace, the King's first response is to say that he expected Da Gama the day before! The king asks why, given Da Gama claims to come from such a rich kingdom, did he bring nothing? Da Gama says that the aim of his voyage was 'merely to make discoveries'. To which the king's acerbic response is to ask Da Gama what he had come to discover: stones or men?! And if it was men that he was hoping to discover, then why had he brought nothing? It was not just Kings who looked down on Da Gama's gifts. They describe being visited at Rio dos Bons Signaes by two gentlemen: 'They were very haughty, and valued nothing which we gave them. One of them wore a *touca*, with a fringe embroidered in silk, and the other a cap of green satin' (p. 20). These kinds of challenges to preconceptions of rich, sophisticated, advanced Europeans discovering lands filled with poor, unsophisticated savages run throughout the original accounts of the journeys. Yet these original accounts have often been erased in the myth-making processes that have transformed these very human men into exceptional heroes.

Returning to the myths made about Vasco Da Gama and more broadly about the origins and true essence of geography, including those reproduced in Livingstone's account, we might ask: to what extent is Vasco Da Gama a geographer? In what ways do his journeys contribute to geographical knowledge? Why is he credited with having 'stunning navigational skills'? What does it mean to 'stake a claim in India'? Who or what gives any right to claim this kind of thing? What might the story look like if 'he' is replaced with 'they'? That is, what if the role of the Gujarati navigator who was actually responsible for navigating Da Gama across the Arabian Sea and the Indian Ocean becomes a part of the stories that we tell?

One answer to the first of these questions – about the extent to which Da Gama is a geographer, and the nature of geographical work that he is doing through these journeys – is found in the move to tie up geography with experiencing the world. For example, and staying with Livingstone's account, experience is given the main role in geography in opposition to theory, positioning experience – touching and feeling the real world – as one response to what Livingstone describes as the 'intellectual crisis' within modern geography. He emphasises the:

> fundamental importance of real-world experience over against the 'authority' of the Greeks. Whether or not there was a southern landmass, or whether the earth was flat, or whether the Atlantic was navigable were questions that could not be resolved by reading Aristotle; they could only be answered by honest-to-goodness experience. The fact that geography has always been a practical science is thus of central significance in its history, and all the more so because the triumph of experience over authority is seen by many as the fundamental ingredient in the emergence of experimental science in the West.
>
> (Livingstone, 1992, p. 33)

Questions about geography's true essence and its origin are part of questions about epistemology, or knowledge. How is geographical knowledge produced? What types of questions are geographers interested in asking and answering? What kinds of knowledge are seen as valid and authentic in geography? What kind of contribution does geography make to human understandings of the world? Early responses to these questions in accounts of geography's history often prioritise experiential knowledge. Seeing, holding, weighing and measuring. This 'honest-to-goodness experience' is the priority, which Livingstone contrasts against types of knowledge that might come from 'authority'. Who is doing the seeing, holding, weighing and measuring becomes an interesting question, with the answer often being that the knowledge forged by the brave lone male explorer is a kind of gold standard. But deconstructing *who* is doing the knowing means that the supposed distinction between authority and experience quickly becomes less clear than might be first imagined. The stories about geography's origins do often construct a lone hero narrative: a man standing on the prow of a ship, wiping sweat from their brow and gazing into the distant horizon. This same man who, so the stories say, later returns victorious having furthered the good and righteous causes of civilisation, justice and peace, benefiting the Crown and their own purse.

> This is a history that tends to be dominated by the actions of European and American men, venturing forth on incredible journeys, either surviving against the odds or being martyred in the process: Dr Livingstone, I presume?
> (Driver, 2013, p. 420)

Failure, disgrace and human complexity are often erased from these stories. Other types of knowledge – particularly testimonial knowledge and Indigenous knowledges – are also erased, such as in the brief example above which showed whose expertise gets recorded and venerated for history: not the Gujarati navigator who actually led Da Gama from Malindi to Calicut, but instead we read of Da Gama's 'stunning navigational skills'. There are some fascinating tensions between the assumptions of geographical knowledge being purely rational and about 'honest to goodness experience' and the ways in which other kinds of knowledges are not only relied on but also deeply affect these adventurers. Portuguese explorations were driven by multiple interests, and their accounts highlight the emphasis given to signs about their possible success. The storm Dias faced is 'only-too-auspicious', whereas the stories about Prester John's presence are enough to bring them to tears of joy:

> We were told, moreover, that Prester John resided not far from this place; that he held many cities along the coast, and that the inhabitants of those cities were great merchants and owned big ships. The residence of Prester John was said to be far in the interior, and could be reached only on the back of camels. These Moors had also brought hither two Christian captives from India. This information, and many other things which we heard, rendered us so happy that we cried with joy, and prayed God to grant us health, so that we might behold what we so much desired.
> (p. 24)

Searches for the elusive Prester John pop up across travel accounts of the period. These searches were elusive because he was a figment of the imagination; a legendary Christian King ruling over an isolated Christian nation surrounded by 'pagans and Muslims' in the Orient. Was he a descendant of the Three Wise Men of Epiphany? Did he rule Ethiopia? Another story told by the Bishop of Acre in 1221 described how Prester John's grandson was King David of India who had conquered Persia and would rebuild Jerusalem. There was some truth in this account because there was a ruler who had conquered Persia. But this was no grandson of a mythical Christian king: it was Genghis Khan. The geographies of this information, and its journeys across time and space are an important subject for geographical exploration and are revisited in Chapter 6.

Joseph Conrad

The year is now 1889, and a Polish sailor – Konrad Korzeniowski – sails to Congo, intending to stay for three years to captain steamboats on the Congo river. However, after one journey from Kinshasa to Kisangani he left, having seen in Congo 'a European regime of appalling greed, violence, and hypocrisy [he] left Africa in a state of psychological and moral despair' (Jasanoff, 2017, p. 3). Later – 1899 – and now living in England with the Anglicised name Joseph Conrad, he publishes the novel *Heart of Darkness* which continues to make lists of 'top 100 best novels.[4] Inspiring Ernest Hemingway, Scott Fitzgerald and others, Jasanoff describes how 'as an immigrant, a traveller, and, not least, a writer in his non-native language, Conrad has been at once a model and a bête noir to postcolonial authors from Achebe to V.S. Naipaul' (p. 314). We will return to Achebe. As a child, Conrad embodies the archetypal geographer, thrilled by the 'discovery of the taste for pouring over land and sea maps'. Writing in the *National Geographic* in 1924, Conrad describes being enthralled by McClintock's book *The Voyage of the Fox in the Arctic Seas* which 'records with manly simplicity the tragic ending of a great tale'. The book is about the expedition of the ships HMS Erebus and HMS Terror. In classic geographic adventure mythology, the leading 'good man' has fame 'rest[ing] not only on the extent of his discoveries, but on professional prestige and high personal character. This great navigator, who never returned home, served geography even in his death'. Conrad is absolutely hooked by the 'breadth of the stern romance of polar exploration', and the 'great spirit of the realities of the story sent [him] off on the romantic explorations of my inner self; to the discovery of the taste for poring over land and sea maps'. He described being entranced by the 'white heart' of Africa – a blank area on the map – putting his finger on it and telling his classmates (much to their derision) that he would go there. Words repeated by his character Marlow:

> Now when I was a little chap I had a passion for maps. I would look for hours at South America, or Africa, or Australia, and lose myself in all the glories of exploration. At that time there were many blank spaces on the earth, and when I saw one that looked particularly inviting on a map (but they all look that) I would put my finger on it and say 'When I grow up I will go there.
> (*Heart of Darkness*, p. 10)

His old atlas, published in 1852, did not mention the Great Lakes: instead, 'the heart of its Africa was white and big' (Conrad, 1924). Since Marlow's/Conrad's childhood, the space on the map had been filled in; rivers named, borders drawn and countries labelled. European imperialism was in full exploration and extraction mode. 'It had ceased to be a blank space of delightful mystery – a white patch for a boy to dream gloriously over. It had become a place of darkness' (Heart of Darkness, p. 11). There is no separation between representation and reality: 'It' had ceased; 'It' had become. The map and the land fused. White gaze erasing black lives. The positioning of subject and object, the gaze of a child: whole continents a boy's plaything. Having proclaimed his dream to one day fill in the map and stand in central Africa, Conrad/Marlow is horrified by what they find. An emotional anti-climax, an illustration of white fragility, and the centring of the heroic lone explorer's personal narrative. Finally reaching the upper Congo, listening as the 'subdued thundering mutter of the Stanley Falls hung in the heavy night air',

> I said to myself with awe, "This is the very spot of my boyish boast." A great melancholy descended on me. Yes: this was the very spot. But there was no shadowy friend to stand by my side in the night of the enormous wilderness, no great haunting memory, but only the unholy recollection of a prosaic newspaper stunt and the distasteful knowledge of the vilest scramble for loot that ever disfigured the history of human conscience and geographical exploration. What an end of the idealized realities of a boy's daydreams!
>
> (Conrad, 1924)

He sees geographical exploration as something good, but which has been disfigured by its close association with violent colonialism. In the background is a true geography, although interestingly this vision of an ideal geography was not something that Conrad recalled from his own school days:

> Unfortunately, the marks awarded for that subject were almost as few as the hours apportioned to it in the school curriculum by persons of no romantic sense for the real, ignorant of the great possibilities of active life; with no desire for struggle, no notion of the wide spaces of the world – mere bored professors, in fact, who were not only middle-aged, but looked to me as if they had never been young. And their geography was very much like themselves, a bloodless thing, with a dry skin covering a repulsive armature of uninteresting bones.
>
> (Conrad, 1924)

Harsh words. So, if he did not discover the true essence of geography from his teachers, who did introduce him to it? In true epic-explorer mode, he describes the way in which he

> discovered for [himself]...the geography of open spaces and wide horizons, built up on men's devoted work in the open air, the geography still militant, but already conscious of its approaching end with the death of the last great explorer. The antagonism was radical.

Conrad's view of geography is as a subject that 'finds its origin in action' (1924). But what kinds of action? The geography of Conrad's time has some deep associations with Empire-building as an imperial subject to the extent that by the late

1850s, 'the Royal Geographical Society more perfectly represented British expansionism in all its facets than any other institution in the nation' (Stafford, 1989, pp. 211–212). Yet Conrad's critique of European imperialism is stinging. In many places, he is far from praising the expansion of Empire but instead takes a hard ethical stance to denounce imperial extraction. In the example above, he describes it as the 'vilest scramble for loot that ever disfigured the history of human conscience and geographical exploration'. Therefore, it might seem surprising for Achebe to describe Conrad as a 'thoroughgoing racist'. Why did Achebe believe that Conrad was racist?

Chinua Achebe is widely considered to be *the* figure of central importance to modern African literature. He was Professor of African Studies at Brown University and won the Man Booker Prize in 2007. I mention all of that to get a sense of the weightiness behind his critique of Conrad. In a 1975 lecture, *An Image of Africa: Racism in Conrad's Heart of Darkness*, Achebe argued that

> the desire – one might indeed say the need – in Western psychology to set up Africa as a foil to Europe, as a place of negations at one remote and vaguely familiar, in comparison with which Europe's own state of spiritual grace will be manifest.
>
> (Referenced here in a later write-up of the lecture; Achebe, 2016, p. 15)

Setting up Africa as the antithesis of Europe, the Congo as the antithesis of the Thames, the black woman ('savage and superb, wild-eyed and magnificent') contrasted against the European woman ('with a pale head, floating toward me...a mature capacity for fidelity, for belief, for suffering'), and savage cannibals as the antithesis of European etiquette, Achebe's argument is that Conrad represents Africans as primitive, to the extent that Africans have no traditions of knowledge passed down through the ages. During their journey down the river – and by this point the black men had been working on the boat for six months – Marlow/Conrad remarks that

> I don't think a single one of them had any clear idea of time, as we at the end of countless ages have. They still belonged to the beginnings of time – had no inherited experience to teach them as it were.
>
> (Conrad, 1899, p. 66)[5]

People and places are described by using Africa as 'setting and backdrop which eliminates the African as human factor. Africa as a metaphysical battlefield devoid of all recognizable humanity, into which the wandering European enters at his peril' (Achebe, 2016, p. 21). The dehumanisation of Africa and Africans that Achebe reads in *Heart of Darkness* leads him to conclude that Conrad was 'a thoroughgoing racist' (p. 21). For a while, 'Conrad saw and condemned the evil of imperial exploitation [he] was strangely unaware of the racism on which it sharpened its iron tooth' (p. 26). Part of Achebe's argument that is particularly relevant to our discussion about exploration and adventure is to do with 'seeing' and the 'blindness' of travellers. Conrad's descriptions of the 'savages' along the banks of the Congo are highly negative – he (or rather a narrator of his story, Marlow) paints a picture of

> hands clapping, of feet stamping, of bodies swaying, of eyes rolling...the black and incomprehensible frenzy. The prehistoric man was cursing us, praying to us, welcoming us – who could tell?...They howled and leaped, and spun, and made horrid faces; but what thrilled you was just the thought of their humanity – like yours – the thought of your remote kinship with this wile and passionate uproar.
>
> (p. 17)

Like rubber-necking a car crash, there is a morbid fascination that thrills the onlooker. The reduction of these humans to close – but below – status next to the Europeans (their humanity is 'like' but not the same; the 'kinship' is 'remote') is at the heart of Achebe's charge of racism. Where others have argued that Marlow is not Conrad, and that Marlow's narration functions as a part of Conrad's critique of European Imperialism, Achebe draws attention to the parallels between Marlow and Conrad's careers, and to the 'advanced and human views' that Marlow offers: perspectives which are 'appropriate to the English liberal tradition which required all Englishman of decency to be deeply shocked by atrocities in Bulgaria or the Congo of King Leopold of the Belgians or wherever' (p. 20). This kind of liberal critique of Imperialism 'took different forms in the minds of different people but almost always managed to sidestep the ultimate question of equality between white people and black people' (p. 20). The 'Heart of Darkness' in Conrad's work is aimed at European imperialism – but as others have suggested, the book is not simply 'anti-imperial' or decolonial. The traveller carries with them the baggage and logic of Empire in the construction and representation of peoples and places. So, although Conrad/Marlow is highly critical of the "noble enterprise" of the Eldorado Exploring Expedition (for example, holding no punches by capturing the aim of the expedition as: "To tear treasure out of the bowels of the land was their desire, with no more moral purpose at the back of it than there is in burglars breaking into a safe"; pp. 31–32), in other ways he is completely blind to the equality, dignity and humanity – let alone to the creativity, invention and sophistication – of the humanity he encounters in Africa. Achebe draws a parallel at this point with Marco Polo. He begins by praising Marco Polo, just as he does Conrad; the latter for their writing skill and the former for being 'one of the greatest and most intrepid travellers of all time' (p. 24). He then goes on to comment on Marco Polo's areas of blindness related the 'two extraordinary omissions in his account'. Printing, a technology that would transform the world (arguably to a greater extent than anything else before or since) did not exist in Europe, but was widespread in China. Yet he doesn't seem to have 'seen' it. In more obviously material terms, the Great

Wall of China was over 1,000 years old when Marco Polo visited, and its incredible 4,500 mile length was far beyond anything built in Europe (even if it is not visible from the moon as Achebe believed[6]). And yet it does not get a mention in Marco Polo's writing: he did not see it. What did Conrad not see?

At the same time that Conrad/Marlow was sailing down the Congo and 'seeing' savages on the banks, something huge was happening in the art world. Picasso, Matisse and others were shown a sculptured mask that left them 'speechless' and 'stunned'. In art historian Frank Willett's terms, 'The revolution of twentieth-century art was under way!' (Willett, 1981, p. 36). This mask, launching cubism and a revolution of European art,[7] was made by people – the Fang people – who lived just north of the River Congo that Conrad describes.[8] And so

> the point of all this is to suggest that Conrad's picture of the peoples of the Congo seems grossly inadequate even at the height of their subjection to the savages of King Leopold's International Association for the Civilization of Central Africa.
>
> (Achebe, 2016, p. 24)

The 'blind' or 'closed-minded' traveller will not 'see' properly, which here contributes to the construction of an Africa – and a Europe – of the imagination. Chakrabarty's hyper-real Europe being deceptively contrasted against its antithesis: Conrad's sub-real Africa.

Exploration by warfare

This phrase – exploration by warfare – is used by Driver (1991) to describe Stanley's expeditions in Africa, referring particularly to his actions at the 'Bumbireh slaughter' and at Victoria Nyanza. By any means necessary this kind of exploration is driven by extraction. From the Village of Kagehyi (near lake Victoria), Stanley wrote letters published in the Daily Telegraph and the New York Herald – also reprinted in the RGS' Proceedings (Stanley, 1875–1876) – giving live updates on the current state of their expeditions.

> We have experienced so much, seen and suffered so much, that I have carefully to recapitulate in my mind, and turn to my note-book often besides, to refresh my recollection of even the principal events of this most long, arduous, and eventful march to the Victoria Lake.

This letter was one of a number, and the connection to the narrative is made for the reader:

> I promised you in my last letter that I would depart as soon as practicable from the old route to Unyanyembe, now so well known, and would, like the

> patriarch Livingstone, strike out a new line to unknown lands. I did so. In our adventurous journey north I imperilled the Expedition, and almost brought it to an untimely end, which, however, happily for me, for you, and for geographers, a kind Providence averted.
>
> (p. 134)

The drama is intense, literally life and death, and the myth-making is dialled up to the maximum: here, aligning with the patriarch Livingstone, who Stanley longingly looked up to and passionately defended. Peril, adventure and striking out to unknown lands, Stanley makes the racialised, classed and gendered nature of the expedition obvious:

> The white men, though elected out of the ordinary class of Englishmen, did their work bravely – nay, I may say heroically. Though suffering from fever and dysentery, insulted by natives, marching under the heat and equatorial rainstorms, they at all times proved themselves of noble, manly natures, stout-hearted, brave, and – better than all – true Christians.
>
> (p. 135)

Mapping, knowing the directions and distances between places, naming those places, drawing borders between them and dividing spaces are powerful actions with potentially world-shaping consequences, and so geography was positioned as central to these national projects of expansion and domination.

> The study and teaching of geography at an advanced level was vigorously promoted at that time largely, if not mainly, to serve the interests of imperialism in its various aspects including territorial acquisition, economic exploitation, militarism and the practice of class and race domination.
>
> (Driver, 1992, p. 141)

Geography was highly effective in serving the interests of imperialism, and Livingstone (1992) identifies two major contributions of geography to the causes of Empire. The first is in terms of shaping understandings and beliefs about the world and its people in racialised, hierarchical terms: a 'moral discourse of climate' (p. 241) in which racist ideas that relate temperature and humidity with intelligence and development are used as the working assumptions to support a 'natural' order of humans. Geography played a significant role in shaping these ideas, and the example of Mackinder's environmental determinism is discussed further in Chapter 3 *Striations of Empire in school geography*. The second area identified by Livingstone is the highly practical training that geography might offer for warfare and militarism, and a symbiotic relationship between the Royal Geographical Society and the British armed forces strengthened both. Not only were geography's beginnings (at least its modern form) in the 1870s in close relation to colonialism and imperialism, but the discipline's service of colonialism also continued. The aims of geography have been explicitly tied up with Imperial expansion, and there are many examples of an intertwining between geographical knowledge, exploration and warfare:

> Vandeleur combined geographical knowledge with military action: 'I never saw him disabled for one moment from taking his sights through his sextant or his equally important sights over the barrel of his Maxim gun,' observed the Company Governor, at a discussion at the Royal Geographical Society, to the presidency of which Goldie was elected in 1905.
>
> (Hicks, 2020, pp. 107–108)

In England, motivation for investing in and promoting geography education was related to national concerns about being 'left very far behind in the field' (Holdich, 1916, p. 180). Holdich (whose full title emphasises the tight connection with the military: Colonel Sir Thomas H. Holdich) was vice-president of the RGS. And this 'being left far behind' particularly involved exposing vulnerabilities through a military disadvantage. And so, Hudson (1972) argues that:

> the armed forces, acting through the Royal geographical Society, where amongst the most energetic champions of advance geographical and education. The strength of military and naval influence in the society in the late nineteenth and early twentieth centuries as indicated by the fact that during that period normally between a third and a half of the 34 council members were officers of the army and navy.
>
> (p. 143)

Having more and better geographical knowledge and skills placed countries at a 'great advantage in negotiations over national spheres of influence and territorial partition' (p. 144). A horrific example of division – from among the many that might be used – is the partition of the Punjab, drawing lines on a map between India and Pakistan/Bangladesh.[9] It is also worth considering the whitewashed ways in which these geographies and histories have often been presented in Britain. For example, Newsround – the BBC's news programme and online resource aimed at children – describes Partition as a 'very important moment in history' that happened when 'British India won its independence from the British and split into two states that would rule themselves'.[10] The article boldly states that 'Newsround takes a look at exactly what happened and what impact it had on people living there.' *Exactly* what happened? The video explainer frames the explanation in a way that paints a picture of India as a multicultural utopia under British rule: 'Before Partition: lots people from different religions and background'. Cartoon people with big smiles and a range of different clothing – Hindus, Muslims, Sikhs, men and women all happily standing together in front of a map with the Indian subcontinent boldly coloured with the Union Jack flag. The voiceover then tells us that this happy multicultural existence was destroyed: 'when it became independent [the country] split up because there was tension between them'. And the text continues emphasising that 'There are still tensions and divisions in the country… Progress has been made, but just as the country was divided 70 years ago, there are still divisions to this day.' The use of the singular ('country') needs explaining; the absolutist, authoritative framing is misleading ('exactly...'); and whitewashing of British impact on the subcontinent in general and partition in particular is bordering on the ridiculous.[11]

Conclusions

Exploration has played a vital role in geography's story, often relying on myths about lone male explorers boldly navigating around the globe and claiming territory and riches as part of a civilising mission. The brief discussion of some of these narratives in this chapter has opened up critical questions through which the idea of exploration might be reclaimed. The examples of Vasco Da Gama and Joseph Conrad offer some insights into the ways these stories have been shaped. In particular, I have tried to foreground different stories about these journeys; stories about the deep reliance on local information and knowledges that force us to rethink popular myths about the brilliant individuality of these men. Histories of geography continue to use enthusiastic descriptors about their 'navigational skills' and so on. The heavy reliance on local navigators challenges these narratives. The extractive ends, clumsy re-naming, and all-too-human errors that creep into these stories also help to reclaim these stories from their presentation as polished myths to more complex and problematic stories. Woven into these accounts – and particularly through those found in narratives about the history of the discipline – are connections with the true essence of geography. In some cases (such as the brief engagement with Stanley) the connections to the RGS are foregrounded. In others (such as Conrad's reflections on his experiences of school geography), there are enduring questions raised about the nature of geography. That is, to what extent is geography about real-world experience, or theoretical arguments? Accounts around the 1800s and early 1900s often prioritise 'actually being there and seeing', which means that 'armchair geographers' come in for a fairly hard time. However, unpicking some of these early accounts of exploration again makes the story more complicated. The kinds of knowledge that are actually used in the construction of this knowledge draws widely on a far greater range than the assumed narrow focus on empirical data. Through the discussion of exploration and geography I have also highlighted the deeply racialised nature of these accounts. Conrad's example is particularly powerful because of the anti-imperial textures of his arguments. Racist assumptions are so firmly baked into his worldview that he seems blind to them. How might these kinds of assumptions manifest in geography? The next chapter seeks to understand more about the nature of Empire's enduring effects on school geography.

Questions and activities

How would you tell the story of geography's origins? Where does it come from? Who has been important to this history?

How have stories by exploration and geography shaped our understanding of the discipline?

In what ways of colonial logics of extraction influenced the practice and teaching of geography?

What are some alternative narratives about geographies origins that challenge traditional Eurocentric perspectives?

Part of Achebe's argument that is particularly relevant to our discussion about exploration and adventure is to do with 'seeing' and with the 'blindness' of travellers (discussing the examples of Marco Polo and Conrad). Is there anything in this discussion that you had not previously 'seen'? How might we, individually and in geography departments, more intentionally seek out blind spots?

What do others you read, listen to, and 'see' through, themselves see? What are they blind to? Even in portrayals that critique European imperialism, is there a fundamental respect for the equality of all humanity? For an article or a book you have recently read, or maybe a programme or film you have watched, critically revisit it asking: what is it 'blind' to? What does it either not see, or not make visible for others to see?

Research and analyse a colonial adventure story from a non-European perspective. How does this challenge or reinforce traditional narratives about exploration and geography?

Reflecting on your own relationship with the discipline of geography, how might your personal experiences and biases influence your teaching practice? Brainstorm strategies for increasing reflexivity in your teaching.

Notes

1 Penck (1916, p. 227) in Livingstone (1992, p. 249).
2 Authorship attributed to Álvaro Velho, although the manuscript is anonymous. For further discussion see: https://www.loc.gov/item/2021667835/#:~:text=APA%20citation%20style%3A,Gama%20to%20India%2C%20%2D1499%20.
3 https://www.independent.co.uk/voices/mea-culpa-vasco-da-gama-didn-t-go-that-far-a8235591.html
4 The 100 best novels: No 32 – *Heart of Darkness* by Joseph Conrad (1899) | Joseph Conrad | The Guardian.
5 References to *Heart of Darkness* from the electronic version available at: https://www.ibiblio.org/ebooks/Conrad/Heart_Darkness.pdf
6 https://www.scientificamerican.com/article/is-chinas-great-wall-visible-from-space/
7 Writing in the Guardian (https://www.theguardian.com/artanddesign/2004/jul/24/heritage.art), Neil MacGregor argued that: the Benin bronzes [are] some of the greatest achievements of sculpture from any period. The brass plaques were made to be fixed to the palace of the Oba, the king of Benin, one above the other, a display of technological virtuosity and sheer wealth guaranteed to daunt any visitor. At the end of the nineteenth century, the plaques were removed and put in storage while the palace was rebuilt. A British legion, travelling to Benin at a sacred season of the year when such visits were forbidden, was killed, though

not on the orders of the Oba himself. In retaliation, the British mounted a punitive expedition against Benin. Civil order collapsed (Baghdad comes to mind), the plaques and other objects were seized and sold, ultimately winding up in the museums of London, Berlin, Paris and New York. There they caused a sensation. It was a revelation to Western artists and scholars, and above all to the public, that metal work of this refinement had been made in sixteenth-century Africa. Out of the terrible circumstances of the 1897 dispersal, a new, more securely grounded view of Africa and African culture could be formed.

8 And for brief discussion of similar development of art among Indigenous North American peoples, see https://www.theguardian.com/artanddesign/2023/mar/10/empowering-art-review-indigenous-masterworks-full-of-wonder-and-sorrow

9 https://www.newyorker.com/magazine/2015/06/29/the-great-divide-books-dalrymple

10 The Partition of India: What happened? – CBBC Newsround.

11 For example, see Purewal and Newbigin's (2022) deconstruction of five myths about the partition of British India: https://theconversation.com/five-myths-about-the-partition-of-british-india-and-what-really-happened-187131

References

Achebe, C. (2016). An image of Africa: Racism in Conrad's heart of darkness. *The Massachusetts Review, 57*(1), 14–27. doi:10.1353/mar.2016.0003

Castree, N. (2005). *Nature*. New York: Routledge.

Conrad, J. (1899). *Heart of Darkness*. Edinburgh: Blackwood's.

Conrad, J. (1924). Geography and some explorers. *National Geographic*.

Driver, F. (1991). Henry Morton Stanley and his critics: Geography, exploration and empire. *Past & Present, 133*, 134–166.

Driver, F. (1992). Geography's empire: Histories of geographical knowledge. *Environment and Planning D: Society and Space, 10*(1), 23–40.

Driver, F. (2013). Hidden histories made visible? Reflections on a geographical exhibition. *Transactions of the Institute of British Geographers, 38*(3), 420–435. doi:10.1111/j.1475–5661.2012.00529.x

Hicks, D. (2020). *The Brutish Museums: The Benin Bronzes, Colonial Violence and Cultural Restitution*. London: Pluto Press.

Holdich, T. (1916). *Political Frontiers and Boundary Making*. London: Macmillan.

Hudson, B. (1972). The new geography and the new imperialism: 1870–1918. *Antipode, 9*(2), 140–153.

Jasanoff, M. (2017). *The Dawn Watch: Joseph Conrad in a Global World*. London: William Collins.

Livingstone, D. N. (1992). *The Geographical Tradition: Episodes in the History of a Contested Enterprise*. Oxford: Blackwell.

Penck, A. (1916). *Der Krieg un das Stadium der Geographie* (pp. 158–248). Zeitschrift der Gellschaft fur Erdkunde zu Berlin.

Stafford, R. A. (1989). *Scientist of Empire: Sir Roderick Murchinson, Scientific Exploration and Victorian Imperialism*. Cambridge: Cambridge University Press.

Stanley, H. M. (1875–1876). Letters of Mr. H. M. Stanely on his journey to Victoria Nyanza, and circumnavigation of the lake. *Proceedings of the Royal Geographical Society of London, 20*(2), 134–159.

Velho, A. (1500). *Journal of the First Voyage of Vasco da Gama to India, 1497–1499*. London: Hakluyt Society.

Willett, F. (1981). *African Art*. New York: Praeger.

Striations of Empire in school geography

Introduction

Striations are evidence of powerful forces that have been at work. Marks that speak of shaping, gouging and earth-forming. Footprints of a former age whose presence continues to be felt through textures and landforms. Striations are evidence of faults moving, glaciers flowing and forming features of the earth's crust. Reshaped rocks, acting as signposts to the forces to which they have been subjected. Jazeel (2019) describes the 'power laden striations of the colonial archive' (p. 181), arguing that the unidirectionality of power relations between those representing against those represented 'betrays the lasting colonial striations and power relations at large in this globalizing, relational and interdependent world' (p. 199). Just as glaciers flowing over land leave huge scars and change the very shape of the land itself, Jazeel riffs off this metaphor to think through the ways in which the powerful forces of colonialism continue to be felt through the very shape of the socio-politico-economic landscape itself.

> Postcolonial scholarship's diverse strands are perhaps drawn together by a common desire to advance discussions about how society at large might take responsibility for the historical fact and iniquitous effects of colonialism and imperialism. This necessitates that the production of postcolonial geographical knowledge must also negotiate those remains; that is to say, the production of postcolonial geographical knowledge mandates that we are responsible for the ongoing colonial and imperial effects of the geographical knowledge we produce given that we work in a planetary context so striated by colonialism.
> (p. 197)

Questions raised by Jazeel are generated by the ways in which postcolonialism inspires us to think about and navigate the production of knowledge, which is vital, 'given that we work in a planetary context so striated by colonialism' (p. 197). Or, in McKittrick's (2006) words, 'geography, as we know, is always about knowledge.

DOI: 10.4324/9781003321682-3

And the ways in which we know and are taught geography, now, is connected to powerful processes of colonialism, exploration, and conquest' (p. 61). As Radcliffe (2017) argues, these connections extend beyond geography into the instrinsic relationships (or 'co-emergence') between colonialism and modernity. Awareness of the closeness of these relationships helps to shift our analysis to examine colonial power and the colonial present not as exceptions and situated 'elsewhere', but as integral to socio-spatial relations across multiple differentiated terrains and scales' (p. 330).

Our cultures bear the marks of colonialism, and school subjects are not exempt. This chapter asks what kinds of striations we might find on school geography. The theoretical perspectives of postcolonialism that Jazeel writes through help us to read and interpret the often taken-for-granted landscape of school geography in new ways. Just as students taken to a glaciated valley might 'see' the valley in completely new ways after they are equipped with some knowledge of glaciation, so too postcolonialism offers the potential to 'see' taken-for-granted features of the subject in quite different ways. Suddenly the student is transported, imagining vast flows of ice, noticing a roche moutonnée and asking new questions, looking for new evidence. I think that a similar thing happens when we start to uncover the ways in which vast flows of colonialism have passed over disciplines and subjects.[1] So much of the ground on which we stand has been shaped by and continues to hold colonial textures. Assumptions, concepts and even the direction of travel made possible through the passages opened bear the footprints of these powerful forces. What do the striations in school geography tell us about the looming presence of Empire?

I have focused this analysis of the striations of Empire in school geography on an important book by Rex Walford (2001) *Geography in British Schools 1850–2000: Making a World of Difference.* I think it is an important book because of the ways in which it produces an understanding of school geography, a representation created in and forming particular space-times: the picture that it constructs of school geography, and the process through which this picture is constructed, are formative as much as informative. Viewed through the prompts of postcolonialism, the absent-presence of Empire and its shaping influence might be seen in new ways through Walford's book and its representations of school geography. More broadly, Walford is also an important figure in school geography in England and beyond. He continues to be celebrated, including through the Rex Walford Memorial Keynote Lecture held annually at the Geographical Association's conference and through the RGS-IBG Rex Walford Award, which aims to recognise outstanding practice among new teachers. The RGS-IBG website describes how the award reflects 'Rex Walford's passion for training new geography teachers who can inspire their students in their subject, it is awarded for the best scheme of work, set of teaching resources and/or lesson plans…' It goes on to honour Walford as 'a teacher, a natural enthusiast, a leading international name in geography education, a long-serving Fellow of the Royal Geographical Society (with IBG) and one of the first group of Chartered Geographers….'[2] I mention all of this for two reasons: firstly, to emphasise the significance of Rex Walford's contribution to geography education. He, and his legacy, have played an important role in the ways in which the subject has been developed and practiced, which makes it particularly important to engage with, both critically and robustly. Secondly, to make explicit the point that – while I do think it is important to critically analyse the work – my aim is not to dismiss or undermine (let alone 'cancel') the importance of his key work and legacy.

There has been very little critical attention given to Walford's arguments, and I hope this chapter might be taken in the spirit suggested by Driver (1992) in his more general comments about the broader version of this issue:

> Some might regard the lack of sustained critical reflection on geography and empire, in Britain at least, as a sign of the strong hold that the colonial frame of mind has upon the subject. It is as if the writings of our predecessors were so saturated with colonial and imperial themes that to problematise their role is to challenge the very status of the modern discipline. Yet this is perhaps the very thing that needs to be done if geographers are to exploit present intellectual and political opportunities. Such a critique need not result in mere handwringing; indeed, it might point us towards alternative roles for geographers in the future.
>
> (p. 26)

By giving this space to analysis and critique, I hope to shed light on different aspects of the subject and the stories we tell about it that might need to be reclaimed.

School geography 'making a world of difference'

Rex Walford played a huge role in geography teacher education in England and beyond, including through his PGCE geography programme at Cambridge, and his impact on teacher education continues to be memorialised annually through subject associations and learned societies. His research interests included the history of school geography, and student–teachers' beliefs about the nature of geography. Over several decades he asked trainee teachers a basic question: 'What is geography?' The responses he received, and his analysis of these responses give interesting insights into the ways in which ideas about the subject have endured despite being formed in very different policy and curricular contexts. This research has stimulated various other work, including collaborations that I have been involved with, exploring fundamental questions about what geography is through the perceptions of those training to teach geography (Puttick, Paramore, & Gee, 2018). Walford explored the question of what school geography is through a historical lens in *Geography in British Schools* (Walford, 2001). As the back matter describes, 'this is the first book to explore the fascinating story of how geography has grown to be a major subject in the British school curriculum in the past 150 years'. It is a fascinating story, and Walford's contribution tells the story in particular ways that also contribute to the ongoing construction of the narrative. As the sub-title suggests, there is an obvious and strong normative element. The subject has and continues to *make a world of difference*.

What kind of *difference* comes across in the book? What conceptions of 'difference' are argued for and assumed by Walford? The importance of making a contribution to 'the world' comes through strongly, and geography is presented as a force for good in the world. The book is dedicated to Walford's students, 'whose idealism about their vocation to teach geography and belief in the educational value of what they are doing has been a constantly heartening experience' (p. xii). A *constantly* heartening experience. I have not taught on the PGCE course at Oxford for as long as Walford led the Cambridge PGCE geography course. However, even in this shorter period of time I can say that it is not *constantly* heartening! I absolutely love my job, and many of our trainee teachers (or 'interns') are incredible. Inspirational, committed teachers with deep subject knowledge, strong beliefs in social justice and a desire to empower young people through geography: a desire to make a world of difference. However, not everyone completes the course. Across our ITE partnership, school mentors and curriculum tutors occasionally have to make the hard decision not to pass an intern. The wider body of research on race, whiteness and teacher education (Bhopal & Rhamie, 2014; Lander, 2011; Lewis, 2018) should also give us pause for thought. This research suggests that we would be naïve to think that any institution could possibly be faced with *constantly* heartening experiences and teachers. Frustration, laziness, deception, arrogance and more are all inescapable parts of the human experience. Teachers – yes, even geography teachers! – are not exempt from this. Arathi Sriprakash and colleagues' (2022) important arguments in *Learning Whiteness* make the case that Higher Education continues to be complicit in and reproduce whiteness across multiple dimensions, and, again, teacher education is not exempt. This small example of presenting geography trainee teachers in a universal and constantly positive light may be fairly trivial, but is one illustration of the ways in which geography is whitewashed. Geography teaching presented as a force only for good in the world, and with echoes of a colonial portrayal of benevolence: striations that shape the landscape of school geography in normative terms as a good thing run by good people who believe they are doing good.

We might also deconstruct the more obvious whiteness that is communicated through the cover images of the book. Two photographs of geography teaching are presented, one illustrating geography teaching at the earliest points covered by the book – 1850 – and the other a more recent modernised version of the subject – 2000. In the earlier photo a white, male schoolmaster stands looking over his class of 30 or more students (all seem to be white, maybe ten-year-old boys) who are sitting in tiered straight rows, arms folded. Two of the students are at the front of the class, standing at a desk with their hands in piles of something that looks like sand next to a model of sailing and rowing boats. On the blackboard, geographical terms are written in chalk using pristine, joined-up script, neatly underlined: *Land and Water; Hills; Isthmus; Sea; River; Harbour…* This photograph also appears later in the book with the description 'A nineteenth-century geography lesson – note the model which is on the front table' (p. 69). In the other, more recent photograph on the front cover are three blond, white students (possibly two boys and one girl, and older than the students in the first photo; maybe 17 or 18 year olds studying for their 'A' Levels). These students are outside and no teacher is visible. Two are crouching at the edge of a river or lake, holding field measurement instruments in the water. The other student stands, typing on an electronic tablet. There seems to be an allegory communicated by these two adjacent photos: geography has grown up. It has moved beyond the classroom, exploring the real world with teachers taking a backseat and facilitating these direct experiences with the world. It has also diversified: there is now a girl included, and the projection of an exclusively male subject is softened.

There are various photographs throughout *Geography in British Schools*, including whole pages dedicated to geography's 'great men'. There are also other photographs of teachers and geography lessons. All of whom seem to be white. In fact, the only black person photographed seems to be someone described as 'an almost unclad Aboriginal' (pp. 55–56), presented in the discussion of the Collins' *Alternative Geography Readers*. Walford describes how the section on Australia 'begins with a chapter on 'Settlers and Explorers' and a practical, colonial perspective immediately emerges: *Cook made Great Britain a present of an almost unpeopled continent and therefore the next thing to be decided was the use to which it should be put*' (p. 55). Describing this passage as showing a 'practical, colonial perspective' is fascinating. Practical. Why *practical*? Maybe because of the decision that is posed: 'the next thing to be decided…' The arrogance of a person giving a country as 'a present' to another country is staggering. And to frame Australia as 'almost unpeopled' curiously avoids any critical engagement with the people who already lived there, which of course is a key part of colonial narratives about (un) peopled places. Walford goes on to cite a horrendous passage from Colonel Warburton about the natives of Western Australia being the 'very lowest in the scale of humanity, and I cannot conceive how anything could fall much lower' (p. 55). This kind of dehumanising racism (also notice the shift in categories from humans to 'things') is a stain on the history of geography. But it is also more than a stain. The texture of this striation speaks of the colonial assumptions that continue to make up the subject. For example, Walford moves immediately to a defence of the passage: 'these comments are, presumably, injected by the author(s) of the Reader to bring a personal and topical perspective to the evocation of the area' (p. 55). The geographers producing these geographies are to be excused because of their good pedagogical intentions. One geographer given a particularly prominent place in Walford's account is Halford Mackinder, who amongst other things is credited with establishing the subject of geography at Oxford.

Racist geographies of Empire

Walford's praise for Mackinder is gushing. Commenting on Mackinder's (1887) paper *On the Scope and Methods of Geography*, Walford writes that Mackinder's

> advocacy and demonstration of the unity of physical and political (or, as we would now say, human) studies in the subject (illustrated with examples from south-east England) was a defining moment in the history of the emerging discipline and compelling to those who heard it; its brilliance of exposition was matched only by the perfection of its timing.
>
> (p. 65)

These are very strong terms! A defining moment. The brilliance of exposition being matched only by the perfection of timing. Heady stuff indeed. The paper was an address delivered at the evening meeting of the RGS on January 31st, 1887. It has been and continues to be highly influential. It has, in a number of ways, made *a world of difference*. Most recently, Ofsted (the Schools Inspectorate in England) enthusiastically included the paper in their review of research in geography (Ofsted, 2021). They cite the paper to represent work at the turn of the twentieth century which caused a 'shift in focus that promoted the relational nature of the subject. This has remained the view of geographers to the present day'. To cite a paper over 130 years after publication is to do it a great honour and give it a continuing place of importance. To go on to claim that the paper's argument ('the relational nature of the subject') continues to be 'the view of geographers to the present day' is a further endorsement of its content. Geography continues to be constructed as a subject that memorialises and honours Mackinder's geography. But what does Mackinder's paper actually say? What is the nature of the 'relational' geography that it developed? Below I will argue that what Mackinder's paper actually says is fundamentally racist. The relationality promoted, while superficially similar to contemporary calls for greater integration across human and physical dimensions of the subject, is an environmental determinism whose imperial logic drives an explicitly racist agenda. In Kearns' (2021) terms: 'In his own geographical adventuring, Mackinder himself set Black lives far below his own pursuit of geographical glory and those who vaunt his reputation in the spaces of the academy, burnish a glory that was most cruelly won' (p. 4). The continuing uncritical promotion and honouring of Mackinder's work in school geography is deeply problematic, and there is an urgent need to reclaim exploration from its role and function in the Empire that Mackinder worked so hard to promote.

Given the actual content of Mackinder's work that is so enthusiastically endorsed by Walford, a footnoted point about Mackinder being 'controversial' is comically understated. Walford notes that 'two of [Mackinder's] books advanced interesting and controversial geopolitical theories' (p. 66). 'Controversial' seems to be doing an awful lot of heavy lifting. When you look at the footnote, you are confronted with casual references to way in which the arguments Mackinder made in *The geographical pivot of history* can be traced directly to Nazi Germany and *Mein Kampf*:

> H. J. Mackinder's two seminal books on geopolitics were *Britain and the British Seas*...and *Democratic Ideals and Reality: A Study in the politics of Reconstruction*...The latter advanced the theory that whoever controlled the Eurasian heartland would be the dominant world power: written in the aftermath of the First World War, it was said to have been read by Adolf Hitler and to have influenced his thinking about strategy. The idea of the 'heartland' as the key to world power was prominent in the thinking and writing of General Karl Haushofer, a leading academic strategist and student of geopolitics in the interwar period. Haushofer often referred to Mackinder's theories in his teaching and writing and called Mackinder's 1904 paper '*The geographical pivot of history*' 'the greatest of all geographical world views ... a geopolitical masterpiece'. Rudolf Hess, Deputy-Leader of the Nazi Party, studied under Haushofer and it is known that Hess provided some of the key ideas for Hitler's *Mein Kampf*.
>
> (Walford, 2001, p. 71)

The comment's status as only an aside in a footnote hints at the lack of critique of geography's 'great men' that seems to be possible. It hints at the kinds of colonial imaginaries driving the subject, and the absence of decolonial or anti-racist thought. This casual discussion in relation to actual Nazis – including the tone, the defence and the absence of pejorative descriptors – contrasts wildly against the description of the anti-racist thought of a woman later in the book (Dawn Gill). We will return to Gill below in a discussion of the way that Walford focuses on her tone to dismiss the anti-racist geography education she argued for. But here, we have positive terms ('key ideas') for *Mein Kampf*. We have full titles ('General, Deputy-Leader') and endorsements ('leading academic strategist') for literal Nazis. It's baffling: why isn't there any critique? Empire's absent-presence weighs heavy; these striations bear the marks of a brutal colonial logic tied up with environmental determinism and a hierarchy of races. This is obviously not to say that Walford is directly arguing for these things. But I am saying that these landscapes and textures show evidence of a powerful shaping of school geography, including here the role those 'great men' (individually) play, and their protection from critique. Rather than subjecting them to critique, these men – elsewhere including John and Sebastian Cabot, Francis Drake, Sir Walter Raleigh, Christopher Columbus, Vasco da Gama, Ferdinand Magellan – are described as 'national heroes' and 'pioneer explorers':

> Later the travels and adventures of Captain James Cook and other pioneer explorers would add to the canon of exciting stories which would thrill young

> children and inspire some of them to dream of exploring the world themselves and visiting 'foreign parts'.
>
> (p. 18)

To further develop the critical argument about Mackinder that I have briefly outlined above I have given a little space below to examine his paper *On the Scope and Methods of Geography*: this is the paper mentioned above that was so strongly endorsed by Walford and, more recently, Ofsted. The paper begins by making general comments about the interconnections between different areas of geography and arguing for the importance of geography above any other subject. Mackinder then metaphorically sketches some landforms, patterns and processes around England, for example, describing the ways in which

> Into the soft clay the sea has eaten, producing the great inlet of the Thames mouth, and the narrower but more intricate sea-channels which extend from Poole Harbour through the Solent to Spithead, and which ramify into Southampton Water and Portsmouth, Langstone, and Chichester Harbours.
>
> (pp. 149–150)

After describing and classifying various rivers he then moves to ask: 'this being the general anatomy of the land, what has been its influence on man?' (p. 151). The nature of the relationship between the anatomy of land and people is determining: the environment causes distinctive types of people to emerge. The first example is of areas 'cut off' or 'shut in': 'The Fens cut off Norfolk, the Weald forests shut in Kent', which means that the '"men of Norfolk" and the "men of Kent" have been of a remarkably rebellious disposition' (p. 151). The determinism is overt in the growth of London: 'Geographical conditions have determined the greatness of the metropolis' (p. 152). The tight relationship between races and places is related to the ways Mackinder sees groups as being homogenous. For example, he defines 'a community' as 'a group of men having certain characteristics in common' (pp. 156–157), and these communities are of 'different orders – races, nations, provinces, towns' (p. 157). Mackinder's interest focuses on the relationships between 'races' and 'environments', such as asking how the different environments that races are 'exposed' to causes differences in their characteristics, successes and so on. For example, he asks 'How have geographical conditions differentiated the English race in the three environments, Britain, America, and Australia?' (p. 157). There are suggestions at the end of this chapter for deconstructing this question, and also for looking at the ways in which the essentialism around 'races' and 'environments' might continue to be reflected in more recent geography teaching resources. Analysis of this question might highlight the ways in which assumptions about homogenous, identifiable 'races' and 'environments' are necessary to support the colonial logic of Empire which requires distinct people groups that can be arranged into a natural hierarchy. For Mackinder, the natural division between races is literally and physically rooted, for example, in there being such a thing as 'English blood'. He believes the Home Counties is the specific region in which this bloodline has been produced:

> Within this natural region we have the English blood, one fluid, the same down through the centuries, on loan for the moment in the forty million bodies of the present generation.
>
> (Mackinder, 1931, p. 326)

There are many obvious problems with this. Apart from there being no such thing as 'the English blood', claiming the existence of these kinds of 'natural' categories, whether for regions or races, drives a colonial deception that there are more and less developed/intelligent/moral/civilised groups of people. None of these categories are natural. A critique of this kind of classification is expressed well by Chakrabarty in *Provincializing Europe.* Challenging the representation of European 'majorities' against other 'minorities', and the asserted hierarchy between them, he argues that:

> Minority and majority are, as we know, not natural entities; they are constructions. The popular meanings of the words 'majority' and 'minority' are statistical. But the semantic fields of the words contain another idea: of being 'minor' or a 'major' figure in a given context. For example, the Europeans, numerically speaking, are a minority in the total pool of humanity today and have been so for a long while; yet their colonialism in the nineteenth century was based on certain ideas about major and minor. For example, they often assumed that their histories contained the majority instances of norms that every other human society should aspire to; compared to them, others were still the 'minors' for whom they, the 'adults' of the world, had to take charge, and so on.
>
> (p. 100)

Mackinder absolutely subscribes to and promotes this fiction of the English being the adults of the world who, therefore, have a moral duty to take charge of others. He emphasises the naturalness of various things and peoples, drawing heavily on the categories and hierarchies between people that are so well critiqued by Chakrabarty. Mackinder emphasises the naturalness of the location of various centres, illustrated by the example of the trade routes along Northern India at the foot of the Himalayas. He describes the area as a

> natural centre of commerce. It is also the natural base of operations for the Asiatic conqueror, his left flanked by the mountains, his right by the desert, his line of communications secure to the rear. The strategic importance of the region has not escaped the British. Here is Simla, the summer capital of India.
>
> (p. 159)

Just as locations are 'natural', so too is an idea of progress over time. Time plays a distinctive role in Mackinder's worldview, and there are linear assumptions of 'development' throughout his work: civilisations are moving forward at different rates in a race. Walford uncritically describes the way in which this idea of progress has informed curriculum sequencing choices:

> The Southern Continents (Africa, South America, Australia) were studied in the first year (on the premise that they were emptier and thus each able to be 'covered' in a term); in subsequent years there would be study of Asia, North America, Europe and the British Isles in a variety of combinations – but premised on the fact that the more developed a country was the more difficult it would be to understand. The complex, more developed parts of the world would come later in the progression of study, though the same regional approach was applied in each case.
>
> (p. 142)

It seems surprising there is no critique of this, nor recognition of the position from which the geography is produced. It is part of longstanding traditions of geographic thought which have 'incorrectly deemed black populations and their attendant geographies as "ungeographic" and/or philosophically undeveloped' (McKittrick, 2006, p. xiii). Equating 'development' with 'complexity' highlights the partiality of this view, its ignorance about the people found on these 'Southern Continents', and its blindness to questions about values; who defines complexity? Or development? And on what basis? This geography is described as providing a

> knowledge base [that] was complete, if superficial. The drawback, however, was that no matter how carefully and elegantly the textbook writers packaged the material, by the time it reached the notebooks and the minds of 3C or 4X, it was scarcely more than a disjointed collection of phrases, some of which were idiosyncratically memorable for life ('jam-making in the Carse of Gowrie', 'short, sharp summers, and warm, wet winters'..., etc.), others which were speedily confined to oblivion after the relevant examination had been taken.
>
> (Walford, 2001, p. 143)

A different series (by Thomas Pickles, and Preece and Wood) is praised by Walford for being 'well-produced and illustrated with neat maps and diagrams...', seeking

> to offer concrete examples to supplement the factual knowledge they represented but did so, not at length, but only with glancing sentence-long references, since they aimed to be comprehensive in their areal coverage. But, looking back on it, there seems to have been little joy, wonder, imagination or

> stimulation in the geography. The shadow of what was examinable, as well as the economic gloom of the age, had come to colour the aspirations and the nature of what was taught.
>
> (p. 143)

The contrast between that which is seen as important to critique here – compared with the absence of critique aimed at the racist examples I have discussed (and go on to discuss below) – is striking. Across all of these examples there is a similarity of primacy given to pedagogy rather than knowledge. This is significant because of the nature of the highly racialised and racist content that Mackinder presents. Central to this geography is an idea of progress and a race between nations. To win in this race it is necessary to conquer others, and returning to the example of the 'Asiatic conqueror' above:

> A wealthy civilised community is a region tempting to the conqueror. Now conquerors are of two kinds – land-wolves and sea-wolves. How would these respectively gain access to their prey in the Ganges valley?
>
> (p. 158)

The imagery is blunt and unapologetic, forcefully betraying the blindness to the abhorrent political, moral and geographical imaginary that it represents. The paper describes some groups as 'prey' while praising British 'conqueror wolves' for their strength and cunning, and for their wisdom in the location of Shimla. To praise such a paper in the uncritical, gushing terms that Walford offers, and to see the place of honour given to Mackinder's paper in Ofsted's 2021 research report, should give us pause for thought. These are sharp, cruel striations of Empire in school geography, creating a geographical vision of the world that needs to be critiqued and disentangled from the subject, not continued to be praised.

Geography and Eurocentrism

Having given some attention to the geography of Empire constructed by Mackinder, I return to Walford's narration of school geography which begins by locating the subject as a European endeavour flowing from 'natural curiosity' in the exotic:

> The roots of geographical education lie in the natural curiosity that all of us have about places and ways of living other than our own. We know little about the origins of those roots in Asia and Africa but as far as the European experience goes, it may be traced back with certainty to hundreds of years before the birth of Christ. Homer's Odyssey can be regarded as the first book to be mainly about travel, a prime stimulation to geographical study, if not strictly a formal geographical text.
>
> (p. 3)

This brief passage does a lot of rhetorical work. Among other things, it illustrates the representation of geographical knowledge being produced through a Eurocentrism that is based on assumptions that immediately 'others' places and ways of living. It is not with 'our' places and ways of living that geographical education begins its critical exploration, but with 'others'. 'We' are brought into this Eurocentric imagination of the world, in which 'our' philosophies and knowledges are the prism against which 'others' might be understood and judged. The little apparently known about African and Asian geographies shifts silently to 'none' in the book through the absence of any African and Asian geographies or geographers. The Asian-born Christ is smuggled into an implicit association with European history, unwittingly undermining the illusion of absolute distinctions between Asia, Africa and Europe. *The* European experience is used as an unproblematic, singular and readily identifiable category. Walford's construction of *Europe* is a good example of what Chakrabarty (2000) calls the 'hyperreal Europe'. This *Europe* does not exist: it is a fiction that continues to play an important role in the narratives that are told about peoples, nations, histories, academic disciplines and school subjects and will 'continually return to dominate the stories we tell…' (p. 39). One consequence of 'Europe' being mobilised theoretically as the lens through which to understand everything is that other places get described through a narrative of being 'behind' and lacking that which Europe already has. 'The modern' will then continue to be understood 'as a *known history*, something which has *already happened elsewhere*, and which is to be reproduced, mechanically or otherwise, with a local content' (p. 39).

Defending the Empire

The specific example of the British Empire, and colonialism in general, are defended in Walford's work in four main ways, each of which offers an insight into the continuing legacy of Empire in school geography: using rhetoric to sidestep problematic aspects; arguing they were 'a product of their time'; adopting a 'balance sheet' to frame Empire in terms of positives and negatives; and attacking critiques of Empire for 'tone'.

Using rhetoric to sidestep problematic aspects

At points where Walford seems aware of other critiques of the Empire and colonial figures that he defends, Walford often uses a rhetorical trick so that the critique does not need to be faced. This rhetoric minimises racism and imperialism by mentioning them only briefly and through sanitised terms. To give two brief examples, Walford (2001) writes that:

> There is also evidence that not all geography teachers were entirely absorbed by *jingoistic sentiments.*
>
> (p. 12)

> Through the 1980s, the consciousness of many geography teachers was raised on the issue and this helped to stem the more *insensitive expressions of cultural bias* which had previously disfigured some classrooms.
>
> (p. 195)

Referring to colonial violence simply as 'jingoistic sentiments' is a rhetorical trick to minimise the horrors of racism and colonialism; who could really object to sentiments? Can any 'sentiments' possibly be all that bad? Similarly, 'insensitively expressing' something might not be ideal, but it is hardly in the same ballpark as being racist. The next step is to use the now familiar 'not all...' More recently, 'not all...' was used to respond defensively to the MeToo movement: 'not all men' became shorthand for a failure to take seriously and listen too – let alone believe – women reporting abuse they had suffered. Here, 'not all geography teachers', or only 'some classrooms' functions in the same way to avoid taking seriously, listening to or believing accounts of colonial abuse whether historic or continuing through the striations left in school geography. In the case of Walford's descriptions of Mackinder, his (1993) *Geography* article is particularly enthusiastic in its praise, filling the paper with enthusiastic endorsements: 'Sir Halford Mackinder is best known for his geographical writing, but also held views on the teaching of geography which appear remarkably close to the modern global approach' (p. 177), and sub-sections fawn over 'Mackinder's long career'; 'Other prophetic chords'; and encouraging 'Valuing the past'. Here, the rhetorical trick is to offer a half-admission that we might find Mackinder's 'language' problematic, but framed in a deception that this is only a matter of style:

> ...though the language may have an antique ring to it, it may be short-sighted if the wisdom and insights of Mackinder and other 'pioneers' are regarded only as museum-pieces.
>
> (p. 122)

An 'antique ring' completely ignores the kinds of overt racism I discussed above. The racism is rhetorically sidestepped and instead the reader is accused of being 'short-sighted' if they are unable to appreciate this great man. The classed nature of the rhetoric is obvious and pernicious; the descriptions of 'wisdom and insight' from 'pioneers' are positioned as becoming 'only' museum-pieces. Yet only those without appreciation of high culture would fail to recognise the value of the work. The use of museum-piece here might be read at multiple levels because being given places of honour and celebrated in museums is never – as those on the inside of the joke know – something the colonial officer class would regard as 'only'.

To give a different example of the ways Walford uses rhetoric to sidestep problematic aspects, in a discussion of *Clyde's School Geography* Walford offers a gentle critique simply as 'unflattering':

> The same willingness of the author to chance his arm in unflattering descriptions of other nations and races remains. In the section on Iberia, Clyde comments, 'The same indolence clings to the Portuguese as to the Spaniard; and if the former wants the pride of the latter, neither is he so manly.'
>
> (p. 41)

The jokey description of the author 'chancing his arm' positions Clyde as just 'a bit of a lad'; oh, funny old Clyde! Yet 'unflattering' hardly seems critical enough for reproducing tropes about the populations of whole countries. This is not serious geographical analysis, and the absence of any kind of rigour is far too easily accepted. Yet these generalisations about whole countries and regions play a key part in the colonial narratives that defend what Hicks (2020) more accurately refers to as colonial *ultraviolence*. The colonial narratives reproduced by Walford (2001) rely on generalisations at a national level, working to sketch a sanitised view of the British and a derogatory view of others. For example:

> The Victorians basked in the unprecedented expansion and growing influence of the British Empire. The map was quickly being 'coloured red' as trade and settlement followed the flag and merchants and emigrants followed British explorers to all parts of the globe. Canada and Australia experienced unprecedented population growth from British migrants in mid-century; the British Raj in India was being formed as a powerful unifying force over many smaller fiefdoms; the 'scramble for Africa' resulted in European powers making many territorial acquisitions in that continent with the British and French the leading colonial powers among them.
>
> (p. 49)

'Basking' is passive, as if this phenomenon were naturally occurring. *The people basked in the morning light as the sun climbed higher in the sky*. Rather than the unprecedented expansion being something actively – and literally – fought for, it is pictured as something natural that just happened to be occurring. The order and list that follows is comical; flag, merchants, emigrants and British explorers. Soldiers and the army are not explicitly listed. Why might that be? Neither are the private militarised industrialists, the archetype of which is the East India Company; for example, see Dalrymple's (2019) *The Anarchy: the relentless rise of the East India Company*, the title of which gives an idea about their approach towards governance. In stark contrast to Dalrymple's analysis of the period, Walford presents a naïve, whitewashed description that positions the British as 'unifying' against 'many smaller fiefdoms'. These kinds of metaphors and descriptions are part of what needs to be de-colonised. Part of what reclaiming exploration means is more honestly facing up to and reclaiming these ways of describing the history of geography and the ways in which it has been implicated (including in a continuing, ongoing way through these kinds of descriptions) in shaping the discursive landscape of school geography. It is about identifying and responding to striations of Empire: here, generalisations about whole countries that position Britain and its history in a passive orientation towards the 'natural' expansion of its Empire.

The use of the passive 'resulted in' from the "scramble for Africa' resulted in European powers making many territorial acquisitions in that continent' does similar rhetorical work. Rather than critically analysing the production of geographical imaginaries through a discourse of 'scramble for Africa', the phrase is used as if it is unproblematic and followed with 'resulted in'. This was not a passive thing or process! It did not simply 'result in'. Even the way in which the militarised theft of land, peoples and property is described follows the same pernicious pattern of rhetorically softening the horror. In the place of a negative descriptor (for example, we might say stole, extracted, or robbed), colonial ultraviolence is described as a positive, constructive process of *making*: 'making many territorial acquisitions'. Throughout, the positive framing softens any sense of deep unease which we might otherwise feel: the subtle message imprinted in Walford's account of school geography is that British colonialism was a good and natural thing.

Balance sheets

At points where the goodness of British colonialism is slightly and lightly questioned by Walford, these negatives are immediately countered by positives. This balance-sheet approach moves very quickly from (still sanitised) negative to positives; to a 'Yet...' For example:

> Victorian society was certainly gripped with a sense of its own social superiority and some of its outpourings about 'natives' and 'savages' sit curiously with professed Christian ideals and the supposed beneficence of the ruling colonial classes. Yet there was also much altruism and idealism mixed with these attitudes, and probably as many migrant [sic] gave 'service' to their fellow human-beings in Empire (for instance, by improving health and educational standards) as oppressed them, or 'destroyed' their culture, knowingly or otherwise.
>
> (p. 53)

The 'probably' is doing an awful lot of heavy lifting, and I am fascinated about the use of scare quotes around 'destroyed'. Is the implication that they were not actually destroyed? Is the conclusion that British colonialism killed 100 million Indians over 40 years[3] just fake news? Or if not, was the process actually doing them a favour; being incorporated into a glorious Empire and being given freedom far outweighs the previous 'culture' or 'lives' which can only benefit from this positive relationship? The shift to defence is rapid, and there is no time to understand the basis on which any of these arguments are made. Who is suggesting there is a 'supposed beneficence of the ruling colonial classes'? There is a wealth of evidence to suggest that beneficence is not an accurate description for a great number of these 'classes'.[4] Railways are the classic trump card in a balance sheet approach to defending colonialism: don't worry about the extraction, murder and theft – look at the railways! As if the balance sheet were dealing with things of the same category: reducing everything to monetary value, the costs and benefits can simply be calculated. The result of the calculation – whether colonial rule caused an increase or decrease in the total – can then be used to judge if it was A Good Thing. A literal balance sheet, listing positives and negatives against each other continues to be used in discussions around school geography. Quoting from Robbins' *The Railway Age*, Walford argues that

> railways by British engineers' acted as 'cement' to bind the 'disparate communities of new colonial possessions...The idea of a Cape-to-Cairo railway, though it remained an idea, was conceived by Cecil Rhodes as the high-water mark of later nineteenth century British imperialism...The nineteenth-century revolution in transportation was the catalyst for the creation of the British Empire – or at least for its transformation into a place which was reachable by ordinary folk; where they might visit or perhaps go to serve a humanitarian or missionary cause for some years, or migrate and carve out a new life for themselves...The same railways which allowed administrators, doctors, teachers, and law-enforcers to travel between widely spaced locations also brought a greater freedom of travel to the inhabitants who previously might not have stirred many miles from their own village.
>
> (p. 52)

The foregrounding of 'humanitarian or missionary cause' is telling; a part of the benevolent white saviour notion of Empire that Walford – and this form of school geography – promotes.[5] This British Empire brings freedom, framing the inhabitants as being given 'freedom' from a previously static life, having been trapped and unable to have 'stirred many miles from their own village'. 'Stirred'? Is the implication they were literally asleep? The lazy native strikes again, just as the prioritising of administrators, doctors and teachers serves to reinforce the benevolence of the whole enterprise. We were there to help! Again we might ask, why is there no mention of the movement of armies? Or the railway's function in maximising the extraction of resources? In Hicks' (2020) terms, these kinds of descriptions have 'continued the trend of not just finding it hard to describe these forms of colonialism, but of neglecting the crucial questions of the scale of violence, of environmental destruction, and of race thinking' (p. 55).

A product of their time?

The fourth tool that I want to suggest Walford uses in his defence of the British Empire and colonialism in general is through appealing to the norms of the time. It might sound racist *now*, but things were different *then*. This argument has been at the heart of defences made of slave traders and the public debates about whether statues of them should be taken down. Where the Rhodes Must Fall movement has argued that we have a moral duty to remove statues memorialising Rhodes (particularly statues in South Africa and Oxford),[6] others have argued that he was simply a product of his time and so his racism should just be put to one side. Walford's comments about Mackinder's language having an 'antique ring' to it are driven by the same logic: don't judge yesterday's writers by today's standards. One obvious problem with this kind of defence is that some things are obviously always wrong, no matter what the 'norms' of particular cultures might say. It has always been morally wrong to regard, or to treat, Black people as inferior or sub-human. Being friends with other racists who thought the same as you does nothing to justify these beliefs and actions, whether then or now. Another problem facing this argument about justifying certain beliefs because they were just a 'product of their time' is that on closer inspection 'their time' turns out to be far more complicated than is implied. The 'product of their time' argument relies on the same kind of ideas that I critiqued above about there being a set of clearly identifiable, homogenous, whole-group (or here, whole time-period) characteristics or beliefs. There might be some trends that we can identify, and there might be some widely held assumptions that we can associate with certain periods of time. However, this only works at the most general, vague level of abstraction. There are always counter-examples, counter-discourses and independence of thought: we are talking about humans. As a book written for teachers, I assume that I don't need to spend much time persuading you that people will think differently about things they are told, no matter how clearly you think you have explained them! Whether these are simple instructions or complex explanations of geographical concepts, how young people understand them, how these understandings interact with their previous knowledge, what they end up rememberingand how these fragments relate to their ongoing experiences, all mean that the direction in which the information they are presented with can – and will – diverge with pretty striking results. It is naïve to think that whole periods of time can possibly force or imprison people to think exactly the same thing. Our geographical analyses need to take seriously the ways in which peoples' agency is real and active. In the case of Rhodes' and Mackinder's racist hierarchies, there are very strong counter-examples to show that everyone at the time most definitely did not hold the same racist beliefs. Both were directly confronted with anti-racist arguments, and contemporaries embarked on completely different projects when faced with the exploitative expansion of Empire. Their racism was not inevitable. Concluding that they were simply passive prisoners of their environment also perpetuates exactly the kinds of environmental determinism that Mackinder developed and promoted. The great men of geography are to be praised and listened to; anything we might now see as problematic should be blamed on their environment. To give a different example of Walford's use of a 'product of their time' argument, he comments that Fairgrieve and Young's position

> predates by some 30 years the British Empire's transformation into a Commonwealth of equals. A relatively enlightened internationalism infused Imperial sentiments for a good proportion of geography teachers, though some were, inevitably, prisoners of the prevailing mood of their time.
>
> (p. 12)

Discussing the school textbook *Geography and History* from 1790, Walford quotes from the chapter on Arabia:

> The Arabians are of middle stature, thin and of swarthy complexion, with black hair and black eyes. They are swift of foot, excellent horsemen, expert at the bow and lance, good marksmen and are said to be a very brave people... The Arabians are in general such thieves, that travellers and pilgrims, who are led thither from all parts through motives of devotion or curiosity, are struck with terror on their approach towards the deserts...
>
> (p. 22)

And in response to this, Walford's view is that

> this description appears to mix fearless reporting with breathtaking judgementalism...hardly an enlightened multi-cultural approach – but it must be seen in the context of its time. At this stage in history, all nations saw each other in terms of distinct 'other-ness' and 'strangeness' and it makes limited sense to apply indiscriminately a twenty-first century set of values in an instinctive vilification of these remarks. Rather, the comments need to be explored for their origins and some understanding given of how they came to be made: they show how insular people generally were, how little they knew of each other and how far away the world was from being a 'global village' at this time....'
>
> (p. 22)

The defence begins from the assumption that these geographical authors are good, and school geography has good intentions to do a world of good. Working from this starting point, a brief, soft critique is immediately followed by defence: *but it must be seen in the context of its time*. Any further critique is dismissed as being 'an indiscriminate vilification'. Again, the same determinism is used to excuse and explain-away the racist tropes that were meant to pass for serious geographical analysis. The same determinism that is used to categorise peoples and create racist hierarchies is used here to clear these geographers from any wrongdoing. The comments do not (we are told) reflect on them, but instead on *their time*: how insular people generally were, how little they knew of each other...' The move to generalisations (generally...) is far too quick and unevidenced.

Attacking critiques of Empire for 'tone'

Maybe we should say that Walford was a prisoner of the prevailing mood of his time. There *was* less geography education research critically engaging with Empire, race and decolonial thought than we have now. However, that would be to deny the geographical scholarship critically examining empire that did exist, and which did come to radically different conclusions; particularly the kinds of scholarship from Global Majority scholars that is notably absent from *School Geography in Britain*. Where Walford does engage with critiques of Empire, he weaponises 'tone' so that the substance of arguments is ignored, instead focusing on how they are presented. This pattern is noticeable in the examples above where a racist description is justified as mixing 'fearless reporting with breathtaking judgementalism', and any potential critiques are pre-empted as being 'an indiscriminate vilification'. Characterising critique as *indiscriminate vilification* is to focus on tone. Of course, the implication goes, critique of these great men would only happen by people reduced to vilifying: being indiscriminate means they are unable to discriminate, but would only deal in generalisations that apply judgements to homogenous groups. The irony is excruciating as we bring to mind the racist tropes indiscriminately vilifying 'Arabians' as thieves (and this just one example among many); descriptions Walford is so quick to defend.

Being quick to defend those responsible for developing racist colonial geographies contrasts strongly with the way that Walford focuses on tone when discussing 'radical' critiques. Chapter 9 of *Geography in British Schools* is titled *Radical Responses, 1975–1985*. After briefly surveying some trends in academic geography, such as David Harvey's *Social Justice in the City*, and the launch of the journal *Antipode*, Walford discusses Dave Hicks' analysis of school geography textbooks. In this analysis Hicks locates textbooks on a diagram running from racist to anti-racist along the X axis, and from Radical to Status quo along the Y axis. It is immediately clear that Walford is unhappy about the study: Hicks' 'study had been thorough, but, of course, the overall judgement about the books was a subjective one. Some authors found themselves unfavourably classified in print, without a chance to respond or explain concerning their books' (p. 186). The irony – again – is heavy to bear! These people are literally authors. They are more than able to respond in print. The point is ironic because these authors were being critiqued for doing the very same thing: for unfavourably classifying whole people groups and nations who are not given a chance to respond.

Walford goes on to argue that this approach of rigorously analysing textbooks and classifying them from racist to anti-racist was problematic because of the way 'unconsciously it set some precedents for later debates when the temperature on the issues raised in the article was raised (many would say justifiably) and judgements about attitudes and intentions thrown about with abandon' (p. 187). Here, temperature = tone. To those able to play the colonial game of adhering to proper etiquette, racism and violence are easily excused. Those unable or unwilling to play this game – those whose outrage at that very same racism and violence is expressed in the 'wrong' way – find that their contributions are dismissed as being emotional and irrational. Calm down, dear! And so Walford claims that 'Many teachers felt that the GA document brought a calmer tone to the rather frenetic arguments which had characterised the 'GYSL [Geography for the Young School Leaver] affair' (p. 195). Instead of articulating and justifying their arguments, they are accused of 'throwing about with abandon': these people, so the implication goes, are irrational and uncivilised. Where the GYSL is praised for being widespread in London schools, those articulating critiques are dismissed for their 'complex ideological arguments'. Only one side is political, ideological and extreme. The other is impartial, objective and rational:

> The heavy political baggage which came to surround the Gill report and the subsequent imbroglio with the GYSL camp was counterproductive in producing immediate educational change. Many teachers who acknowledged the cogency and legitimacy of some of Gill's criticisms of school materials did not necessarily share the radical and Marxist-inspired analysis of education which accompanied them. The highly politicised context recruited some enthusiasts to the cause, but the strident and indiscriminate tone of later criticisms alienated other possible supporters. The original basic concerns (notably the need to develop multicultural perspectives in geography teaching) became bound up in complex ideological arguments which did little to advance day-to-day work in schools.
>
> (p. 192)

There is also an irony in the sense discussed above: strident and indiscriminate accurately describe the colonial geographies defended by Walford, yet those colonial geographies are not subjected to similar critique for tone, or to charges of having 'heavy political baggage'.

As part of the rhetorical strategy of focusing on tone, Gill[7] is isolated so that even those making similar arguments are positioned in a way that undermines Gill's position. For example, Walford argues that 'Huckle had been a discerning commentator from the left on geographical educational issues for some years and had provided a probing but less overtly aggressive view about what went on in school classrooms' (p. 191). Even when a letter co-authored with Ian Cook is discussed, Walford describes Cook not simply as a co-author but as 'an academic geographer who had been *drawn into* the argument' (p. 190, italics added). Much of the attention given to Gill surrounds her critique of the teaching resources produced through the GYSL project, which alford describes as 'immensely successful...whose well-produced materials were widespread in London schools' (p. 190). He goes so far as to claim that it was the success of the project – rather than any Eurocentrism or racism perpetuated through the resources – that was responsible for its 'undoing':

> Many schoolroom resources stem from particular attitudes and viewpoints not shared by the teacher or the school (newspaper articles being an obvious example); in the hands of skilful teachers, such attitudes are exposed and discussed and the resource evaluated as well as put to use. But the widespread success of GYSL in geography classrooms was its undoing; it tended to make those suspicious of it act in a confrontational manner.
>
> (p. 190)

Walford also reproduces the GYSL response, noting that

> GYSL did, in fact eventually withdraw the material which was under criticism, but maintained that, 'Our line has always been that teachers are intelligent beings, capable of using such materials with care.' They acknowledged gaucheries and language deficiencies in some of their early work sheets while stoutly resisting a charge of racism.
>
> (p. 190)

Gaucheries and language deficiencies: categories that overlap with the tactics discussed above designed to minimise and soften the charge. Where the GYSL authors are given the description of 'stoutly resisting', those offering a critique exposing the racist assumptions in some of the materials are radical, strident and indiscriminate, or extreme radical: 'Whilst extreme radical conclusions were not generally accepted, the general analysis which lay behind them often was' (p. 195) – *of course* we are not disagreeing with any facts, or when presented with rational analysis. We are perfectly reasonable, and so *of course* we cannot accept any extreme radical conclusions. The construction is also curious; extreme radical. Extreme and radical? British geography racist? WHAT! How dare you, you EXTREME RADICAL. It is telling that Mackinder and others are not labelled in this way.

Conclusions

In this chapter I have tried to take up Jazeel's metaphor of 'striations' to explore the ways in which school geography bears the imprints of Empire, and I have done this through a slightly extended analysis of the ways in which Rex Walford narrates the story of school geography in his book *Geography in British Schools 1850–2000: Making a World of Difference.* My main argument in this chapter has been that the school geography constructed through *Geography in British Schools* bears the marks of Empire through colonial assumptions that whitewash geography's past and pay insufficient attention to confronting the racist ways in which the subject has treated people and places. The continuing uncritical use of Halford Mackinder's work, including through the English schools' inspectorate Ofsted, highlights the enduring legacy of these arguments that bind geography with the colonial imperative. Jazeel's (2019) prompts to ask 'In what sense are we actually after, or beyond, the subjugating effects of colonial power? And, in what ways can we thus think against the grain of colonial power's lingering effects both at home and abroad?' (p. 5) suggest positive, proactive responses – a thinking against the grain. My hope is that the critical discussion of Walford's *Geography in British Schools* in this chapter makes the shape and textures of this grain a little clearer. The next chapter – *Power and Prisoners* – continues this work of exploring the striations of Empire in school geography by pushing some of these arguments a little further in the contexts of discussions around Powerful Knowledge and *Prisoners of Geography*.

Questions and activities

What does the metaphor of striations mean and how does Jazeel apply it to the study of colonialism? To what extent do you think it applies to an analysis of geography education?

Where do you see striations of Empire in the geography teaching you have experienced? What voices are included in this geography? What or who is labelled, for example, as 'extreme radicals?' What might be the implications of this labelling?

In what ways can we confront racist assumptions present in the teaching of geography?

Look over a few lesson plans or outlines from the last few weeks of your teaching. Critically review the extent to which they have been sensitive to issues of race and colonialism. How might you challenge students to think more critically about the subject and its history in the context of these particular lessons?

Map out your own journey through the subject of geography. How has your understanding of the subject been shaped by your background and the cultural context in which you grew up?

Choose one of the geography textbooks that you use. Critically analyse it to identify any assumptions or biases that bear the striations of Empire. What changes would you suggest to address these issues?

Use the metaphor of striations to analyse a particular landscape or environment in your local area. What evidence do you see of past or ongoing colonialism and imperialism?

Notes

1 I think this metaphor is useful, but I am also aware that it has limits, particularly the danger of implying that the subject of geography is 'passive' and has been eroded and changed by Empire and colonialism when it has at times actively contributed to the colonial project and might be better seen in this metaphor as glacier than land.
2 https://www.rgs.org/schools/competitions/rex-walford-award/

3 For example, see Sullivan and Hickel's (2022) analysis: https://www.aljazeera.com/opinions/2022/12/2/how-british-colonial-policy-killed-100-million-indians
4 See Lester's summary and response to ideas around 'legacies' of Empire: https://blogs.sussex.ac.uk/snapshotsofempire/2022/10/10/what-are-the-british-empires-legacies/
5 Also see/engage further with *Education, race and empire* (Mitchell, 2017) – relationships between humanitarianism, imperialism, education, race and philanthropy.
6 For example, see Kwoba, Chantiluke, and Nkopo (2020).
7 For wider context around Dawn Gill, Norcup's doctoral thesis offers a fascinating insight into the journal CIGE and sheds light on what had been a largely ignored part of the story of school geography in Britain.

References

Bhopal, K., & Rhamie, J. (2014). Initial teacher training: Understanding 'race,' diversity and inclusion. *Race Ethnicity and Education, 17*(3, SI), 304–325. doi:10.1080/13613324.2013.832920

Chakrabarty, D. (2000). *Provincializing Europe*. Oxford: Princeton University Press.

Dalrymple, W. (2019). *The Anarchy: The Relentless Rise of the East India Company*. London: Bloomsbury.

Driver, F. (1992). Geography's empire: histories of geographucal knowledge, *Enviornment and Planning D Society and Space, 10*(1), 23–40.

Hicks, D. (2020). *The Brutish Museums: The Benin Bronzes, Colonial Violence and Cultural Restitution*. London: Pluto Press.

Jazeel, T. (2019). *Postcolonialism*. Abingdon: Routledge.

Kearns, G. (2021). Topple the racists 2: Decolonising the space and the institutional memory of geography. *Geography, 106*(1), 4–15.

Kwoba, B., Chantiluke, R., & Nkopo, A. (Eds.) (2020). *Rhodes Must Fall: The Struggle to Decolonise the Racist Heart of Empire*. London: Bloomsbury.

Lander, V. (2011). Race, culture and all that: An exploration of the perspectives of White secondary student teachers about race equality issues in their initial teacher education. *Race Ethnicity and Education, 14*(3), 351–364. doi:10.1080/13613324.2010.543389

Lewis, T. E. (2018). 'But I'm not a racist!' Phenomenology, racism, and the body schema in white, pre-service teacher education. *Race Ethnicity and Education, 21*(1), 118–131. doi:10.1080/13613324.2016.1195354

Mackinder, H. J. (1887). On the scope and methods of geography. *Proceedings of the Royal Geographical Society and Monthly Record of Geography, 9*(3), 141–174.

Mackinder, H. J. (1931). The human habitat. *Scottish Geographical Magazine, 47*, 321–335.

McKittrick, K. (2006). *Demonic Grounds: Black Women and the Cartographies of Struggle*. London: University of Minnesota Press.

Mitchell, K. (2017). Education, race and empire: A genealogy of humanitarian governance in the United States. *Transactions of the Institute of British Geographers, 42*(3), 349–362. doi:10.1111/tran.12180

Ofsted. (2021). Research review series: Geography. Retrieved from https://www.gov.uk/government/publications/research-review-series-geography/research-review-series-geography

Puttick, S., Paramore, J., & Gee, N. (2018). A critical account of what 'geography' means to primary trainee teachers in England. *International Research in Geographical and Environmental Education, 27*(2), 165–178. doi:10.1080/10382046.2017.1321304

Radcliffe, S. A. (2017). Decolonising geographical knowledges. *Transactions of the Institute of British Geographers, 42*(3), 329–333. doi:10.1111/tran.12195

Sriprakash, A., Rudolph, S., & Gerrard, J. (2022). *Learning Whiteness: Education and the Settler Colonial State.* London: Pluto Press.

Walford, R. (1993). Mackinder, the GA in wartime and the national curriculum. *Geography, 78*(2), 117–123.

Walford, R. (2001). *Geography in British Schools, 1850–2000: Making a World of Difference.* London: Woburn.

Power, knowledge and prisoners

Introduction

The characters at the heart of the story in Chapter 3 illustrate the importance of power in and for geography. Power of nations, private companies and individuals over others. Epistemological power about what kinds of knowledge are accepted as valid; and political and military power over classifications, land, resources and people. In making an argument about striations of Empire in school geography, I suggested that colonial logics deeply influenced the kinds of geographies and geographers that were valued and celebrated in Walford's influential account. In various ways, we can 'see' the impact of colonial thought on school geography and the arguments used to defend these perspectives. Walford's book reported on school geography 1850–2000, and I now want to extend and update the argument about Empire's deep striations across school geography by critically exploring the more recent ideas of Powerful Knowledge and *Prisoners of Geography*. These two (quite different) influences on school geography – one a concept from the sociology of education, and the other a popular book – have been taken up enthusiastically through many aspects of school geography policy and practice internationally. In both cases, there are important questions to ask about the ways in which they might be critiqued, re-thought and expanded.

Critiques of powerful knowledge

In work with Amber Murrey (Puttick & Murrey, 2020), we described the 'deafening silence' on race in school geography. In making a case for school geography to be enriched through greater engagement with Black and decolonial geographies, we argued that powerful knowledge – even on its own terms – calls for work by academic geographers such as Katherine McKittrick, Tariq Jazeel, Ruth Gilmore, Simon Browne, Patricia Daley and many others to inform the school subject. Our argument was that 'anti-racist geographies provide powerful frameworks to address white supremacy and institutionalised racisms' (p. 126). We did not make a

DOI: 10.4324/9781003321682-4

case against powerful knowledge. Instead, we took the view that while powerful knowledge continues to be a highly influential approach in education, we should recognise that even among the problematic aspects of powerful knowledge (such as those explored further in this chapter), the call from powerful knowledge to value disciplinary knowledge makes it is necessary to engage with anti-racist geographies that have been implicitly and explicitly side-lined and silenced through the implementation of the approach. We argued that 'working *within* powerful knowledge, Black and decolonial geographies bring attention to knowledge creation and the great potential that exists to learn from anti-racist conversations and internal debates within academic geography' (p. 126). The hope of that argument is for a 'more holistic and sustained anti-racist school geography education that empowers young people to understand the complex and shifting politics of space, place and knowledge and to contribute to meaningful anti-racist futures' (p. 126). So, why not leave it there and continue working *within* powerful knowledge?

Since *Confronting the deafening silence on race in geography education in England* was published in 2020 there has been a significant increase in work that is informed by and contributes to anti-racist geographies. We highlighted an extreme situation: the complete absence of race or racism from any formal school geography curricula in England. We pointed out that just one article in the whole of *Teaching Geography*'s back catalogue from 1975 to that point in 2020 explicitly mentioned 'race'. Ironically, the single article in *Teaching Geography* mentioning race was written by Keith Ajegbo (2011) who self-defined within that article as 'not being a geographer'. Since our article was published, attention to issues around race and racism in *Teaching Geography* has increased, including: decolonising initial teacher education (Reilly, 2022); classroom strategies for tackling the whiteness of geography (Milner, 2020); starting conversations about diversity in education (Milner, Robinson, & Garcia, 2021)and more. The *Decolonising Geography* collective[1] have played a significant role in these discussions, critiquing existing curricula and practices and stimulating the development of new resources. There has also been increasingly critical attention given to the idea of powerful knowledge.

Defining powerful knowledge

In the discussion below, I bring some of these arguments together to critique powerful knowledge and suggest that we leave the term behind: I do not think that it is a useful or productive concept to help take the geography teaching adventure forward.

In collaboration with English and Mathematics teacher education colleagues, we have focused on the conceptual issues associated with powerful knowledge (Puttick, Elliott, Ingram, 2023), including the changing ways in which it has been defined. We argued that powerful knowledge is a 'cluster concept'. Wittgenstein uses the idea of cluster concepts to speak about games. What is a game? It eludes a simple propositional statement to define it: some games involve winning, but not all; some are played on boards, others with cards and others with no external objects; some are individual, others are played in teams. Lots of potential aspects of what 'games' involve, none of which are necessary or sufficient on their own. We argue that this means that asking '*shall we play a game?* is one kind of question, but it does not get you much closer to deciding what to do. What type of game? Which game shall we play? What counts as 'a game', and 'what kinds of activities are excluded as not-games?' To give another example, Czocher and Weber (2020) discuss the mathematical idea of 'proof', which they argue should be seen through the idea of a cluster concept. The nature of proof understood as a cluster concept complicates the relationship between disciplinary knowledge and classroom concepts and practices. They argue that:

> [T]he relationship between mathematicians' proving practice and classroom proving processes is not straightforward, and there are good reasons why disciplinary and classroom practices might differ...Nonetheless, most mathematics educators believe that pedagogical goals with respect to proof and the types of proof that we expect students to produce should at least be informed by mathematicians' practice with proof.
>
> (pp. 50–51)

In a similar way, Young does not define powerful knowledge through a proposition that captures the fundamental meaning of the concept. Instead, he offers various lists of things that, individually, are neither sufficient nor necessary (illustrated by his use of terms like 'normally...') to define what 'powerful knowledge' means: each a different dimension of this cluster concept. Without clarity over the concept, it is hard to use in practice. What counts as powerful knowledge, and what knowledge is not powerful? Who gets to decide, and whose knowledge is accepted as legitimate?

In part, these questions about knowledge are about the history of the discipline: a history that is deeply and messily tied up with unequal, extractive colonial logics. And in part, these power relations are about constructing the curriculum. In the context of school geography, who gets to decide what kinds of knowledge count as 'powerful'? Saying that 'disciplinary' knowledge is what counts as powerful knowledge does not work. The discipline is so massive, and so contested, that referring to what 'it' might show us is impractical. The school subject has more specific aims along with temporal and conceptual restrictions. I agree with Bruner that we should be able to teach any idea to anyone at any stage if we use ways that are appropriate for them: 'Any subject can be taught effectively in some intellectually honest form to any child at any stage of development' (Bruner, 1960, p. 33). One pretty solid limitation is time. Geography is often allocated an hour or two each week in schools. What from this 'sprawling, ragged, gorgeous discipline' which 'ranges across the physical and social sciences into the humanities and the performance arts' (Geoghegan et al., 2020, p. 462) might we choose to include within those precious couple of hours?! Through what kinds of processes and pedagogies might we hope to represent this discipline with its 'whole heap of different ways of doing what it does. It maps and models. Critiques and exposes. Drills and digs. Surveys and measures. Talks and hangs out with. Theorises. Analyses. Deconstructs' (p. 462). Geoghegan et al. go on to describe what happens if you ask a group of academic geographers what geography is: 'Each would give a different answer. Stuffy and hip, it's a discipline with too much difference for some and yet not nearly enough for others' (p. 462). We might push their description further but also look backwards to allude to the shadow of the discipline along with all of this shine: it extracts and steals. Controls and divides. Determines, racialises, excludes and others. It has the potential for so much harm but also for so much healing. By taking an uncritical stance towards disciplines, powerful knowledge does not create the space necessary to open these conversations about the kinds of knowledges that are most worth teachers' and students' time. Catling and Martin explicitly say that while their arguments are made in the context of geography, they also apply across the whole of primary education. There are subject-specific aspects of these questions about the definition and concept of 'powerful knowledge' that geographers may answer differently to those from other subject traditions. For example, see the discussion of the ways in which geography, English and mathematics might understand, justify and speak about knowledge from different perspectives in the collaboration mentioned above (Puttick, Elliott and Ingram, 2023). There are also common themes that apply across subjects; different ways in which the striations of Empire are gouged into and have been forged through historic and ongoing entanglements with extractive colonial logic. The experiences shaping the shadow sides of disciplines and the 'shine' of disciplines are two sides of the same coin and their histories are bound together. Allowing insufficient attention to experience, both of this shadow type but also more generally, is a weakness of powerful knowledge that limits the ways in which the concept might be useful for a geography that is enriched through exploration and adventure: through experiences that are an important part of generating, learning from and wrestling with geographical knowledges.

Knowledge and experience

The problem of side-lining the idea of experience in powerful knowledge was highlighted by Catling and Martin (2011) in one of the earliest critiques of powerful knowledge in geography education. At the heart of their critique is an argument for the importance of pupils' and teachers' everyday knowledges, which they refer to as 'ethno-geographies'. In Martin's terms, ethno-graphy:

> Reflects the view that all [teachers and pupils] are geographers because they all live in the world. The[y] all negotiate and interact with a variety of

> landscapes (human and natural) on a daily basis. Through these daily interactions and decisions they will have built up a wide knowledge base about the world, near and far, through a range of direct and indirect experiences. What they don't perhaps recognise is that this knowledge is useful geographical knowledge and a point from which deeper conceptual understanding can be developed.
>
> (Martin, 2015, p. 291)

The distinction between everyday experience and knowledge made by powerful knowledge is overly simplistic, which Martin illustrates here by touching on the breadth of knowledge that young people have. The connection between experiences (negotiating, interacting and deciding) and the development of knowledge is also interesting in the way that knowledge is seen as 'building up' through these experiences. Martin claims this is useful geographical knowledge. And then the journey of this knowledge continues, and the vertical metaphor is pushed in a different direction from 'building up' from experiences to become geographical knowledge, it is then described as a point from which 'deeper conceptual understanding can be developed'. I like the way in which this journey seems to return to those experiences. They are the basis from which knowledge is built up from, and from those heights of knowledge, the depth of experience is returned to: deeper conceptual understanding. Mapping out the spaces of these knowledge imaginaries would produce some fascinating journeys, but here I want to emphasise the connections between them. Experience, knowledge, understanding, concepts; these spatial metaphors of a young person's journey push us to a networked, interactive perspective. Such a perspective is quite different to the sharp binary through which Young presents knowledge and experience. They go on to push the idea of experience not only as something passive but in a negative way as something that young people need to 'break' away from:

> We have schools, colleges and universities which provide students with opportunities to break with their past experience and begin to trust the possibilities that knowledge and a *knowledge-based* curriculum can offer them.
>
> (p. 20)

The places in which this knowledge is learnt (schools, colleges and universities) are particular kinds of institutions, and the place-based significance of these situated engagements with knowledge again contrasts with the 'placeless' objective knowledge claimed for their idea of powerful knowledge.

In defining experience – that which knowledge is contrasted against – they write that 'experience is just experience – what we are' (p. 18). There is a passiveness to this. Experiences on this view are 'just' received, which is very different to Martin's active descriptors of negotiating, interacting and deciding. There is also a curious reductionism (or determinism?) in the equivalence of experience with 'what we are'. I want to say that we are far more than our experiences. It is not our experiences that make us, but how we respond to them. Their passive view of experience is then contrasted against knowledge which they see as always active: acquiring powerful knowledge 'always requires much dedicated effort and hard work' (p. 18). And so, 'knowledge, like anything worthwhile, is not only shared but has to be struggled for – wrought from the world by work no less dedicated than the work it took to create it' (p. 18). This is obviously not always true: for me to know the height of Everest would take far less dedication than the measuring and so on that it took to create that knowledge. Or to give a more common example, reading a book and writing a book are different and require quite different levels of time and effort (although I appreciate that you might not agree in the case of the book you are currently reading!). To give another example of the profound differences that they want to argue for between everyday experience and powerful knowledge they contrast experiences and knowledge of a city – London:

> [P]upils' relationships with the 'concept' of a city should be different to their relationship with their 'experience' of London as a city where they live. It is important that the pupils do not confuse the London that the geography teacher talks about with the London in which they live. To a certain extent, it is the same city, but the pupils' relationship with it in the two cases is not the same. The London where they live is 'a place of experience'. London as an example of a city is 'an object of thought' or a 'concept'
>
> (p. 98)

By replacing the geographical terms (city, London) with terms drawn from the study of literature (play, *Hamlet*), Eaglestone shows in the context of English as a discipline and school subject 'how bizarre [the concept of powerful knowledge is] for the study of literature' (p. 16). He argues that 'the division between literature as experience and literature as "classroom object" is just incoherent...of course, studying a play develops and deepens a student's knowledge but this knowledge begins in the experience of seeing or reading it' (p. 16). This argument applies well in the context of geography, and to take up the example of the city, there is an important sense in which the city is also something to be firstly experienced and read: of understanding the city as an abstraction, as text (Jazeel, 2021). Jazeel's postcolonial critique in the context of urban studies includes attention (following Spivak, Chakrabarty and others) to individuality and particularity; to provincialising. At the heart of this is a reading of cities 'on terms true to the singularity of their differences' (p. 661). It is not with context-free generalisations that knowledge of the city is only (or even primarily) located. And so the challenges to their conception of the city are multiple: the city as text means, in Eaglestone's terms, that the knowledge of the city 'is in and arises from the personal experience'. The city itself is not a fixed, static 'thing' that exists apart from the lives of the residents (least of all young people in the city), but instead is produced through them – the city is constituted through their relationships, interactions, and so on. This means that these young people's 'experiences' of the city are not something separate from the city – in some senses they *are* the city. There are certainly different ways of looking at, understanding and analysing 'the city', but there do not seem to be any necessary reasons to prioritise one type over another. It takes a kind of reductive scientism to conceptualise the city and knowledge about the city in ways that creates it as something separate from and distinct from the experiences of the young people who live in the city. The places in which these knowledges are produced and connected to are part of shaping the knowledge itself.

Knowledge in places

The challenges of defining knowledge can be illustrated by exploring the ways in which Young's extensive attention to knowledge overwhelmingly defines it negatively. In his view, powerful knowledge is not experience, nor is it 'opinions or common sense'. He also defines it in relation to its features: knowledge is something produced by people, and something that has changed and will continue to develop. In *Knowledge and the Future School*, Young et al.

> start with [the] view that as educators, we must differentiate types of knowledge: in particular between the knowledge that pupils bring to school and the knowledge that the curriculum gives them access to. This view does not involve any esoteric distinctions, nor will it be wholly unfamiliar to readers of this book. Despite this [,] it is all too often dismissed by educationalists.
>
> (p. 14)

This passage immediately illustrates the polemical way in which powerful knowledge has been presented. Who, we might ask, is dismissing knowledge? What 'educationalists' have 'too often' dismissed these things? There are no references to give the reader a hint about who they have in mind and so it is hard to know. Young et al.'s (2015, p. 17) insistence that knowledge and experience are distinct also raises some issues. They argue for knowledge as something *universal* which means that 'unlike common sense [knowledge] is never something 'given' and *never* tied to specific contexts' (p. 17). The polemical language – *never* being tied to a specific context – undermines the point they are trying to make. In what ways might some knowledge not be tied to a specific context? What does it mean to be 'tied' there? There is a strong geographical tradition of exploring the place-based dimension of knowledge – its 'situatedness' – that speaks against a view of knowledge as a view from nowhere, arguing against 'the erroneous belief that, since it can be formalized, codified knowledge is also decontextualized' (Rutten, 2017, p. 161). Recent discussions of climate models are a good example of this argument. The IPCC (Intergovernmental Panel on Climate Change) is the United Nations body for assessing the science related to climate change.[2] Established in 1988, the IPCC has synthesised, summarised and communicated a phenomenal amount of the scientific community's latest understandings of climate change. To put a number on the 'phenomenal' amount of citations to peer-reviewed published research, the 'physical science basis' for climate change ARP6 report published in 2021 included 13,500 references. Currently with 195 members and thousands more who give time to their work, the IPCC reports are designed to 'provide a comprehensive summary of what is known about the drivers of climate change, its impacts and future risks, and how adaptation and mitigation can reduce those risks'. The processes through which these reports are produced are described as being 'open and transparent' leading to 'an objective and complete assessment'. Is this the ultimate example of powerful knowledge that is not tied to a specific context?

Analysis of the IPCC reports suggests that even in this incredible example of international, interdisciplinary collaboration that has played such an important role in our understandings and responses to climate change, describing the knowledge that it produces as being context-free is misleading. There are geographies of knowledge creation for all knowledge: socio-spatial dynamics connecting people, places, networks, institutions, norms, processes and more in complex ways. Rather the producing a 'view from nowhere or anywhere', these models and reports might instead be seen as producing a view from somewhere (Borie et al., 2021). For example, in their discussion of IPCC AR5 (Intergovernmental Panel on Climate Change Assessment Report Five), Ford and colleagues (2012) examine the limited role that indigenous knowledges, understandings and voices had played in IPCC discussions by using the proxy of chapter authorship. Finding that only 2.9% of the chapter authors had published on climate change and indigenous populations, they made suggestions for future recruitment of authors and reviewers bringing more of this expertise. They argue that diversifying the authorship is vital to 'help broaden our understanding of climate change and policy interventions' (p. 201). This broadening is necessary because of the 'training, disciplinary background and positionality' through which authors go about the processes of reviewing and assessing the state of knowledge in specific areas of climate change. These author teams 'decide what research to include and exclude, how much space to allocate to each topic, a structure for framing knowledge and how to deal with conflicting arguments, as well as writing style and language' (Ford et al., 2016, p. 349). Of the 13,500 citations in the ARP6 report, 99.95% were written in English, and 75% of this research had at least one author based in the UK or the US.[3] Borie et al. (2021) push this argument further by analysing the conceptual frameworks, scenarios and consensus produced by the IPCC and IPBES (Intergovernmental science-policy Platform on Biodiversity and Ecosystem Services (IPBES)). Their analysis suggests that the IPCC seeks to present a ' "view from nowhere", through a reliance on mathematical modelling to produce a consensual picture of global climate change', whereas the IPBES' approach of bringing together 'contrasting conceptual frameworks and practices of argumentation, appears to seek a "view from everywhere", inclusive of epistemic plurality, and through which a global picture emerges through an aggregation of more place-based knowledges' (p. 67).

However, neither of these aspirations – whether for a view from nowhere or a view from everywhere – are able to escape from their places which are somewhere. Both organisations offer ' "views from somewhere": situated sets of knowledge marked by politico-epistemic struggles and shaped by the interests, priorities and voices of certain powerful actors' (p. 67).

All of this analysis of the ultimate example of powerful knowledge – international syntheses from thousands of leading experts – opens different kinds of questions about the knowledge itself. Questions about who gets included as the authors, and who in turn these authors choose to cite – which revisits questions above about power relations in terms of who gets to speak, who is represented, and what knowledges are validated through the process. And this is one critique to direct at Young et al.'s claims that knowledge is never tied to specific contexts. Rather, it is always produced in specific contexts. Reclaiming geographical exploration involves rediscovering who and where knowledge was and is produced.

(Powerful) knowledge, truth, beliefs and fear

On this point about knowledge being 'situated', arguments from powerful knowledge have become very concerned about relativism (Wrigley, 2017). If knowledge is constructed by people in particular places, and the knowledge bears the imprints of these places, then how can we know anything for certain? Surely it would be different if it was produced elsewhere, and so we're doomed to clutching at straws? Fear of the ghost of relativism (elsewhere 'postmodernism' is used as the term for this bogeyman) hovers in the background of claims about objectivity and certainty.

Young et al. (2015) assert that knowledge is fallible: 'however true something is it is only the truth as far as we know' (p. 17). Leaving aside the question of how 'true' is being used in this account, the argument continues: 'It is this openness that distinguishes knowledge in the sense used in this book from our everyday experience and lies at the root of its links with freedom; it always opens up new possibilities…' (p. 17). However, there seems to be no reason to assume that 'everyday experience' is held as being non-fallible by anyone. These kinds of straw men appear frequently, including through fictional teachers who apparently avoid the question of knowledge: 'Why is acquiring [knowledge] seen as so problematic and divisive that teachers often avoid the question of knowledge altogether?' (p. 15). They proceed to make the (unsubstantiated) claim that there is a ' "fear or knowledge" often found among teachers' (p. 17). The point of highlighting this is to develop a broader critique of powerful knowledge. Here, the critique is related to the rhetorical, polemical basis of these arguments that too often rely on generating fear about the alternatives, and fear about what others are apparently doing, thinking and believing. Although not given significant attention, another contrast is made between knowledge and belief which illustrates this point: 'We need knowledge to live in a complex world but we cannot live by knowledge – we live by beliefs in what we value which may or not be the beliefs of a religion' (p. 18). They briefly expand on the idea of religion in relation to these claims to state that:

> Although religious ideas are not knowledge in the sense we use the word in this book, they are one of the sets of values which people live by; as educators we must respect such beliefs and values even when we do not share them.
>
> (p. 18)

This gives a fascinating insight into the ways in which Young defines and uses knowledge which elsewhere is foregrounded in relation to his dismissal of 'voice' and postcolonial critiques of knowledge and subjects. The conceptual issues with the way that powerful knowledge is defined return as they grapple with ideas around truth and knowledge:

> Like knowledge, truth is another difficult and misunderstood word and certainly we do not mean truth in an absolute sense. We mean the best truth a student can grasp depending on their age and development. Furthermore, truth is like knowledge; it is differentiated and may be scientific, aesthetic, moral or practical. Somehow, as teachers, in whatever we ask our students to do – there should be some idea in our mind that it has a 'truthful' outcome or challenge to existing ideas – it might be about a poem, a historical source or the property of a chemical element.
>
> (p. 26)

Here, the ghost of 'absolute truth' is ducked, while un-named others who 'misunderstand' truth are addressed and then avoided. The same pattern of defining negatively (not truth in an absolute sense) also seems to limit the conceptual clarity of the discussion. The subject-specific examples they offer – a poem, historical source and property of a chemical element – each bring their respective subject traditions' perspectives of disciplinary understandings of and engagements with these things: methods of reasoning, justifying and accepting particular kinds of understandings and of shaping the kinds of questions that are seen as worth pursuing. I now move to develop a geographical critique of the kinds of understandings promoted in *Prisoners of Geography*.

Critiquing *Prisoners of Geography*

Prisoners of Geography opens with these words:

> Vladimir Putin says he is a religious man, a great supporter of the Russian Orthodox Church. If so, he may well go to bed each night, say his prayers and ask God: 'Why didn't you put some mountains in Ukraine?'
>
> If God had built mountains in Ukraine, then the great expanse of flatland that is the North European Plain would not be such encouraging territory

> from which to attack Russia repeatedly. As it is, Putin has no choice: he must at least attempt to control the flatlands to the west.
>
> (Marshall, 2016, p. ix)

'Putin has no choice'. This cuts immediately to the heart of my critique of *Prisoners of Geography*: this is wrong, because humans – including Putin – do have choices. It has always been true that people have choices, however much these choices might interact with multiple complex and conflicting topographical, psychological, moral, spiritual, emotional, climatological, relational, ideological and other factors. Part of the wonder of geography has been exploring, mapping, analysing and deconstructing this vast array of relationships, networks, dimensions, structures and agents. The geographical project has generated profound and fascinating insights into the ways in which peoples, technologies, environments, more-than-human actors, concepts, theories and representations produce time-spaces. Part of this discussion of *Prisoners of Geography* is specific to this book and the kinds of environmental determinism that it fosters, and part of this argument is broader: it is about the potential for geographical analysis as a generative tool through which to read and see other popular books about geography. Books that might offer seductively simple accounts of the world and its peoples, cultures, natures and communities that we might use in productive ways by bringing disciplinary insights to bear.

Mackinder's deception (discussed in Chapter 3) gives the impression of ambition and profundity of thought by cutting through irreducible complexity by telling massive but reductionist and racist stories at a global scale. It is a deception because geopolitics, population distribution and human–nature relationships are far more complicated than this. Even putting the overt racism and Empire-building to one side, Mackinder's geographical project is far too simplistic. My argument is that *Prisoners of Geography* replicates an environmental determinism that strongly echoes Mackinder's geographical imagination, and in doing so it suffers from the same kind of over-simplicity. Yes, landscapes are important. The presence – or absence – of mountains makes a difference. But so do lots of other factors, and they are also not (only or even primarily) important in the way that Marshall and Mackinder imagine them to be. Both Marshall and Mackinder underestimate the function that representation has on the production of landscapes. Mountains are not just there, existing as an objective fact. They are also epistemological and exist in ways that are built up through collective meaning-making. As Macfarlane (2003) puts it,

> What we call a mountain is thus in fact a collaboration of the physical forms of the world with the imagination of humans – a mountain of the mind... Mountains are only contingencies of geography...But they are also the products of human perception; they have been imagined into existence down the centuries.
>
> (p. 19)

Mountains are not (only) lines on a map. Because the representation – or the imaginative production – of landscapes is so important, the adjectives and metaphors through which we do this work of representation is powerful. Their vision of the relationships between humans and landscapes produces a world in which landscapes imprison people; people who have little or no agency (or the corollaries of freedom, dignity and responsibility). *Prisoners* of Geography might be eye-catching and help to sell books (the copy I bought from Oxfam announces that it is 'The International and *Sunday Times* bestseller'), but it is a woefully narrow and dangerously misleading idea with origins in the same kind of environmental determinism that is a long way from current geographical understandings and analysis. I say this is dangerous because of the close association between these assumptions about who is 'really' from this place, racism and xenophobia.

But where are you *really* from?

We're in Buckingham Palace, and it's 2021. Ngozi Fulani has been invited to an event designed to raise awareness about gender-based violence. She has been invited in her role as Chief Executive of Sistah Space,[4] a charity supporting women and girls of African heritage who have suffered domestic abuse. Other useful background information: Fulani is from London. She was born in Brent, grew up in Kilburn and went to South Kilburn High School. She went to college in Hackney and after that studied for a BA and then an MA from SOAS, University of London. Fairly strong London theme. Back to Buckingham Palace – less than two miles from SOAS, and only eight miles from where Fulani was born – she is confronted by the late queen's 'lady-in-waiting' (Susan Hussey). Hussey repeatedly asks Fulani where she 'really came from'.[5] The conversation is below as Fulani described it,[6] and which Hussey does not contest; she apologised and resigned for it. SH is Susan Hussey, and NF Ngozi Fulani:

SH: Where are you from?

NF: Sistah Space.

SH: No, where do you come from?

NF: We're based in Hackney.

SH: No, what part of Africa are YOU from?

NF: I don't know, they didn't leave any records.

SH: Well, you must know where you're from, I spent time in France. Where are you from?

NF: Here, UK

SH: NO, but what Nationality are you?

NF: I am born here and am British.

SH: No, but where do you really come from, where do your people come from?

NF: 'My people', lady, what is this?

SH: Oh I can see I am going to have a challenge getting you to say where you're from. When did you first come here?

NF: Lady! I am a British national, my parents came here in the 50s when …

SH: Oh, I knew we'd get there in the end, you're Caribbean!

NF: No Lady, I am of African heritage, Caribbean descent and British nationality.

SH: Oh, so you're from…

One of the assumptions driving Hussey's line of questioning is that there are visible markers that connect a person's physical appearance in an obvious way to a place. You're not from here: when did you first come here? The most obvious marker is probably skin colour. As Paul Gilroy (2002) puts it: *There Ain't No Black in the Union Jack*. In that same book he argues that while

> the nascent global culture of human rights has achieved a great deal in a short period, it has not always been alert to the significance of either colonial domination or racism as tests of its own lofty aspirations and cosmopolitan conceptions of justice.
>
> (p. xv)

The 'Buckingham Palace Incident' illustrates this with a sad irony. The lofty aspirations of raising awareness about gender-based violence is blind to the 'significance of either colonial domination or racism'; tests that are both failed as the pernicious assumptions about race and nation surface. What are you really from?

In the case of *Prisoners of Geography*, homogenising, static assumptions about peoples and nations comes through in the descriptions on Europe's 'traditional white' and 'indigenous population':

> Europe's traditional white population is greying. Population projections predict an inverted pyramid, with older people at the top and fewer younger people to look after them or pay taxes. However, such forecasts have not made a dent in the strength of anti-immigration feeling among what was previously the indigenous population, which struggles to deal with the rapid changes to the world in which it grew up.
>
> (Marshall, 2016, p. 108)

I feel that we need to insert massive scare quotes – the kind drawn emphatically with a fat Sharpie – around "traditional white population" and around the "indigenous population." What does 'indigenous' mean? And does it describe people in Europe? In the example of England, we are back to Mackinder's ideology of race and his 'pure English blood' concentrated in the Home Counties. The idea of being a separated island contributes to the myth of being 'an island race':

> Geographically, the Brits are in a good place. Good farmland, decent rivers, excellent access to the seas and their fish stocks, close enough to the European Continent to trade and yet protected by dint of being an island race – there have been times when the UK gave thanks for its geography as wars and revolutions swept over its neighbours...
>
> (p. 105)

After the 2011 census, public discussion around the term 'Indigenous' was amplified when Paul Collier misleadingly claimed that the 2011 census in England revealed that "indigenous" Britons had declined as a percentage to the extent that they were now a minority in London.[7] This was misleading because the census actually showed that 63% of London's population had been born in England.[8] But that detail aside, his use of "indigenous" – like Marshall's – is also misleading. The then chief executive of the Runnymede Trust, Halima Begum, criticised the association of Indigenous with white British by linking it to the ways in which far-right extremists have weaponised this language: 'referring to indigenous Britons, which is a proxy for white Britons, is the incredibly divisive language used by the British National Party in the 1980s.' But what does Indigenous mean?

In Marshall's use of 'indigenous', it means something like 'the original dwellers on the land'. It is used to construct ideas of being the true inhabitants and the rightful owners. Whoever has been there the longest is the 'indigenous' one. However, this is a subtle sleight of hand; a pernicious move to locate whiteness in relation claims about race and nation that misuse the term. Across policy (such as the UN's use of indigenous), and geographical analyses (For example, see: Radcliffe, 2016), the concept of Indigenous peoples (and indigeneity) has a very different meaning that is bound up with ideas about power, coloniality and Western modernity. To begin with the policy example, the United Nations Permanent Forum on Indigenous Issues[9] locates indigenous peoples cross the globe from the Arctic to the South Pacific, giving as illustrative examples the Lakota, Mayas, Inuit, Aborigines, Maori and others:

> Practicing unique traditions, they retain social, cultural, economic and political characteristics that are distinct from those of the dominant societies in which they live...The new arrivals later became dominant through conquest, occupation, settlement or other means.

Following this description, it is clear why they do not include 'English' among the examples of Indigenous peoples. Most significantly, the power relation that is necessary for an understanding of indigeneity is missing: what is the 'dominant society' against which this 'Indigenous' population might be defined? Yet this is precisely the point of the trick. To stoke fears of invasion, domination, occupation and settlement: *they* are going to take *your* land. Yet the kinds of 'traditional white people' invoked by Marshall, Collier and Mackinder – if we accept for the purposes of argument this deeply problematic grouping – are the dominant society: they are the colonial power. Asking what kind of unique traditions and distinctive characteristics might we point to also highlights the inappropriateness of using 'Indigenous' to refer to the English because the deeply and historically multicultural nature of England defies this kind of homogenous identifier.

Moving to geographical analyses of Indigenous peoples and indigeneity, Radcliffe (2016) pushes these arguments further by highlighting how:

> authenticity and 'prior presence' are less relevant than the forms of power and economy that produce indigeneity continuously in relation to non-Indigenous subjects, sovereignty, environment, the academy, and policy.
>
> (p. 226)

Being 'Indigenous' is a status that is produced through colonial relations: it emerges through 'colonial histories, postcolonial modernities' and is a 'relational reading and a producing of difference...that is always embedded in power differentials at multiple scales' (p. 221). Rather than being simply 'the first ones', the concept of 'Indigenous people' instead emerges differently in different places through contested processes and always through power asymmetries, having a historical continuity with pre-colonial/pre-settler societies. Therefore, co-opting the term 'Indigenous' to refer to the white population in England is deeply problematic. It is a form of cultural appropriation, stealing the term and pretending that the power imbalances are flipped and the colonial histories are inverted. Yet Marshall does not make this argument explicit. Instead, indigenous is used as a subtler move that pretends to be innocent to the wider political associations of the term. It is a simplistic account of people and places that is underpinned by problematic assumptions about 'race', nations and geography. Where are you *really* from? With depressing inevitability, the descriptions of Africa in *Prisoners of Geography* illustrate these issues further.

Africa

Before making a helpful point about the ways in which the Mercator projection has warped ideas about the size of Africa, Marshall opens with this description of Africa:

> Africa's coastline? Great beaches, really, really lovely beaches, but terrible natural harbours. Rivers? Amazing rivers, but most of them are rubbish for actually transporting anything, given that every few miles you go over a waterfall.

> These are just two in a long list of problems which help explain why Africa isn't technologically or politically as successful as Western Europe or North America.
>
> (p. 116)

Immediately, these aspects of the physical geography of the continent are foregrounded to explain 'why Africa isn't technologically or politically as successful as Western Europe or North America'. Framing this as a 'long list of problems' – and particularly placing these physical features at the top – is problematic for a number of reasons, but I will suggest just three: firstly, it's a wild oversimplification to say the natural harbours are terrible, and the rivers are rubbish for transportation. The hugely 'efficient' and 'successful' slave trade is a tragic illustration of the argument that 'natural' infrastructure exists to support huge industry; secondly, the timeline is too short and so the description hides the fact that for a huge swathe of human history the 'success' both technologically and politically was greater than that in Western Europe or North America (for example, see the discussion above around the way in which Da Gama's gifts were received and what this implies about the relative wealth and sophistication of the societies); thirdly, emphasising 'natural' features above the historic and enduring role of colonial extraction from the continent reduces the overwhelmingly negative impact of colonialism in constructing current ideas about the 'success' or otherwise of the continent, or in other words *How Europe Underdeveloped Africa* (Rodney, 2018).

Continuing these negative descriptions of Africa, Marshall asserts that 'there are lots of places that have been unsuccessful, but few have been as unsuccessful as Africa' (p. 116). It's hard to overstate the extent to which this is poor geographical analysis and unworthy of being given valuable curriculum time in classrooms. The deficit narrative that it constructs begs so many questions about what counts as success, who decides, and to what extent generalisations at the continental level can give us anything meaningful. The notion of 'success' that Marshall uses is tied up with ideas about time, history and progress which present the journeys of peoples and nations through time as one of a competition or race:

> ...despite having a head start as the place where *Homo sapiens* originated about 200,000 years ago. As that most lucid of writers, Jared Diamond, put it in a brilliant National Geographic article in 2005, 'It's the opposite of what one would expect from the runner first off the block.' However, the first runners became separated from everyone else by the Sahara Desert and the Indian and Atlantic oceans. Almost the entire continent developed in isolation from the Eurasian land mass, where ideas and technology were exchanged from east to west, and west to east, but not from north to south.
>
> (p. 116)

This image of Africa as being separated and developing in isolation is repeated for emphasis:

> Africa, being a huge continent, has always consisted of different regions, climates and cultures, but what they all had in common was their isolation from each other and the outside world. That is less the case now, but the legacy remains.
>
> (p. 116)

But this is just not true. This representation merely repeats lazy myths that ignore the substantial trade and exchange (economic, intellectual, cultural) that existed within and beyond Africa for thousands of years. This approach ignores 'Africa's global interactions from the very distant past...In Western discourse, either exclusionary language is used for 'Africa' (Africa is "without history" or "without modernity")' (Green, 2019, p. xx). After briefly mentioning some of the sophisticated trading histories, and the written and oral accounts of these narratives, Green's view is that 'this is such a rich and complex subject. It defies generalization...' (p. xxii). There is enduring epistemic violence committed through the imposition of Eurocentric knowledge systems and the 'thing-ification' of Africans (Daley & Murrey, 2022). Vital words that are at the heart of the critical questions that I want to raise about *Prisoners of Geography*: this richness, complexity and particularity should not be flattened or written out of our geographical understanding and analysis. There are also strong parallels with Chakrabarty's critique in *Prozincializing Europe* discussed above in which the myth of a hyper-real Europe is used as the marker against which others are judged. Marshall's account continues to use a racing notion of 'head start' but this time negatively to frame a claim about the disease:

> But Africa's head start in our mutual story did allow it more time to develop something else which to this day holds it back: a virulent set of diseases, such as malaria and yellow fever, brought on by the heat and now complicated by crowded living conditions and poor healthcare infrastructure...
>
> (p. 116)

This is the same kind of racism that saw COVID-19 described as the 'Chinese virus' and was associated with increases in Asian hate crimes in North America[10] and globally, to the extent that police in England reported a tripling of hate crime towards Asians in the first three months of 2020.[11] An Africa not only 'dark' but dirty and disease-ridden. And what is meant by 'it' developed these things? Again, this is not a useful geographical analysis of health or disease, particularly when the origins of so many diseases are from temperate regions, with more temperate diseases being acute than tropical, and most temperate diseases being 'crowd epidemic diseases' (for example, measles, rubella and pertussis). Through their review analysing the origins of major human infectious diseases, Wolfe and colleagues (2007) flip the narrative about Africa being the major cause of diseases to instead associate 'modern developments' such as industrial food production as increasing vulnerability to new pathogens. They also make a brief historical argument about the ways in which diseases have been circulated, and the impacts of the introduction of new diseases to areas:

> Far more Native Americans resisting European colonists died of newly introduced Old World diseases than of sword and bullet wounds. Those invisible agents of New World conquest were Old World microbes to which Europeans had both some acquired immunity based on individual exposure and some genetic resistance based on population exposure over time, but to which previously unexposed Native American populations had no immunity or resistance.
>
> (pp. 281–282)[12]

Just as topography does not play a necessary or deterministic role in development or geopolitics, neither does disease. Political decisions and framings of these things mean that they are constructed in particular ways that enable them to be described, used, governed and weaponised for different ends. More broadly, geographical analysis of health strongly indicates that there is nothing at all 'natural' about the wild differences in life expectancy and access to health care: disasters are not natural (Puttick, Bosher, & Chmutina, 2018). Instead, these inequalities are gendered, classed and racialised in ways that are all too familiar (Dorling, 2013). Framing questions about power, development, technology, disease, culture (and more) in deterministic terms – as things that people are 'prisoners' to because of their 'geography' – is to completely misunderstand the nature of these things, the nature of the people, the nature of history, and the nature of geography itself. The geography is far richer and more complex than these reductionist accounts allow, and the stories are much better even if they cannot be captured in snappy soundbites about whole continents.

Conclusions

Both the concept of powerful knowledge and the book *Prisoners of Geography* ambitiously offer big stories, whether about knowledge or the world. One common thread that I have followed in the critiques above is connected to the ways in which they treat (or rather, to the ways in which they minimise and ignore) 'shadow' sides to these projects. Shadow related to Empire and colonial extraction as an aspect of knowledge and academic disciplines (particularly through some of the ways in which geographical knowledge has been produced in service of Empire), and as a key dimension through which we might understand the 'development' and the stories that we tell about the development of countries and continents. In both accounts, my argument is that geography is tied up in messy ways with these attempts to know, describe and rule the world. And yet in both accounts, a reclaimed notion of geographical exploration also offers the tools to introduce students to far richer and more complex understandings. In the case of powerful knowledge, reframing the engagement with the discipline in ways that allow both shadow and shine to be critically examined opens questions about geography's problematic past and lays the foundation for building more equitable and inclusive futures. In the case of *Prisoners of Geography*, the ghost of Mackinder's environmental determinism continues to haunt the account. In both cases, reframing the engagement with geography is vital so that fuller accounts of people and places can emerge; reframing the engagement with the discipline in ways that equip students to question these simplistic stories about peoples and nations. The truth is far more interesting and empowering.

Questions and activities

Who decides what knowledge is seen as legitimate in the context of school geography, and what are the implications of these decisions?

Critically review the arguments about powerful knowledge made in this chapter. What is your view on the suggestion to replace it with the idea of disciplinary knowledge?

How can teachers more effectively represent the sprawling, ragged and gorgeous discipline of geography within limited class time?

What are the ethical implications of using disciplinary knowledge in the classroom, especially in the context of the discipline of geography's past engagements with unequal extractive colonial logics?

As a department, choose a sequence of lessons or a scheme of work. Collectively analyse the types of knowledge that are being prioritised through these lessons, then reflect on the potential ethical implications of these choices. In what ways might these lessons better reflect the complex nature of the discipline?

Review the arguments about the use of 'Indigenous'. What are the implications of using the term to describe dominant people groups?

Notes

1 Decolonising Geography (decolonisegeography.com).
2 About—IPCC. https://www.ipcc.ch/about/
3 https://www.carbonbrief.org/guest-post-what-13500-citations-reveal-about-the-ipccs-climate-science-report
4 https://www.sistahspace.org
5 https://www.theguardian.com/uk-news/2022/nov/30/buckingham-palace-aide-resigns-black-guest-traumatised-by-repeated-questioning
6 https://twitter.com/Sistah_Space/status/1597854380115767296?s=20
7 https://www.independent.co.uk/news/uk/politics/michael-gove-levelling-up-paul-collier-b2010396.html
8 https://www.ons.gov.uk/census/2011census

9 https://www.un.org/esa/socdev/unpfii/documents/5session_factsheet1.pdf
10 https://www.bbc.co.uk/news/world-us-canada-56218684
11 https://www.theguardian.com/world/2020/may/13/anti-asian-hate-crimes-up-21-in-uk-during-coronavirus-crisis
12 Wolfe, Dunavan, and Diamond (2007) use 'Old World' to refer to Africa, Asia and Europe and 'New World' to refer to elsewhere.

References

Ajegbo, K. (2011). Diversity, citizenship and cohesion. *Teaching Geography, 36*(2), 46–48.

Borie, M., Mahony, M., Obermeister, N., & Hulme, M. (2021). Knowing like a global expert organization: Comparative insights from the IPCC and IPBES. *Global Environmental Change, 68*, 1–14. doi:10.1016/j.gloenvcha.2021.102261

Bruner, J. (1960). *The Process of Education*. Cambridge, MA: Harvard University Press.

Catling, S., & Martin, F. (2011). Contesting powerful knowledge: The primary geography curriculum as an articulation between academic and children's (ethno-) geographies. *Curriculum Journal, 22*(3), 317–335. doi:10.1080/09585176.2011.601624

Czocher, J. A., & Weber, K. (2020). Proof as a cluster category. *Journal for Research in Mathematics Education, 51*(1), 50–74.

Daley, P. O., & Murrey, A. (2022). Defiant scholarship: Dismantling coloniality in contemporary African geographies. *Singapore Journal of Tropical Geography, 43*(2), 159–176.

Dorling, D. (2013). *Unequal Health: The Scandal of Our Times*. Bristol: Policy Press.

Ford, J. D., Cameron, L., Rubis, J., Maillet, M., Nakashima, D., Willox, A. C., & Pearce, T. (2016). Including indigenous knowledge and experience in IPCC assessment reports. *Nature Climate Change, 6*(4), 349–353. doi:10.1038/nclimate2954

Ford, J. D., Vanderbilt, W., & Berrang-Ford, L. (2012). Authorship in IPCC AR5 and its implications for content: Climate change and indigenous populations in WGII. *Clim Change, 113*(2), 201–213. doi:10.1007/s10584-011-0350-z

Geoghegan, H., Hall, S. M., Latham, A., & Leyland, J. (2020). Continuing conversations: Reflections on the role and future of area from the new editorial team. *Area, 52*(3), 462–463. doi:10.1111/area.12642

Gilroy, P. (2002). *There Ain't No Black in the Union Jack: The Cultural Politics of Race and Nation*. Abingdon: Routledge.

Green, T. (2019). *A Fistful of Shells: West Africa from the Rise of the Slave Trave to the Age of Revolution*. London: Penguin.

Jazeel, T. (2021). The 'city' as text. *International Journal of Urban and Regional Research, 45*(4), 658–662. doi:10.1111/1468-2427.13029

Macfarlane, R. (2003). *Mountains of the Mind: A History of a Fascination*. London: Granta Books.

Marshall, T. (2016). *Prisoners of Geography: Ten Maps That Tell You Everything You Need to Know about Global Politics*. London: Elliott & Thompson.

Martin, F. (2015). *The relationship between beginning teachers' prior conceptions of geography, knowledge and pedagogy and their development as teachers of primary geography*. (PhD). Coventry.

Milner, C. (2020). Classroom strategies for tackling the whiteness of geography. *Teaching Geography, 45*(3), 105–107.

Milner, C., Robinson, H., & Garcia, H. (2021). How to start a conversation about diversity in education. *Teaching Geography, 46*(2), 59–60.

Puttick, S., Bosher, L., & Chmutina, K. (2018). Disasters are not natural. *Teaching Geography, 43*(3), 118–120.

Puttick, S., Elliott, V., & Ingram, J. (2023). *Knowledge, Keywords in Teacher Education*. London: Bloomsbury.

Puttick, S., & Murrey, A. (2020). Confronting the deafening silence on race in geography education in England: Learning from anti-racist, decolonial and Black geographies. *Geography, 105*(3), 126–134.

Radcliffe, S. A. (2016). Geography and indigeneity I. *Progress in Human Geography, 41*(2), 220–229. doi:10.1177/0309132515612952

Reilly, S. (2022). Supporting trainee teachers to decolonise the school geography curriculum. *Teaching Geography, 47*(2), 64–66.

Rodney, W. (2018). *How Europe Underdeveloped Africa*. London: Verso Books.

Rutten, R. (2017). Beyond proximities: The socio-spatial dynamics of knowledge creation. *Progress in Human Geography, 41*(2), 159–177. doi:10.1177/0309132516629003

Wolfe, N. D., Dunavan, C. P., & Diamond, J. (2007). Origins of major human infectious diseases. *Nature, 447*(7142), 279–283. doi:10.1038/nature05775

Wrigley, T. (2017). 'Knowledge', curriculum and social justice. *The Curriculum Journal, 29*(1), 4–24. doi:10.1080/09585176.2017.1370381

Young, M., Lambert, D., Roberts, C., & Roberts, M. (2015). *Knowledge and the Future School: Curriculum and Social Justice*. London: Bloomsbury.

5 Journeys of information

Introduction

Moving beyond the examples of *Prisoners of Geography* and the concept of powerful knowledge, this chapter extends the discussion about the information that reaches school classrooms. Exploring information through its consumption, circulation and production is to go on a geographical adventure fit for the twenty-first century. This chapter also takes forward the ideas about engaging with the academic discipline of geography and developing generative interactions across these spaces: the geographies of information are here seen as a curricular resource, topic and inspiration for further research and geographical enquiry. The fundamental questions driving this interest are illustrated through the vignette below: through what kind of journeys does information travel into school geography classrooms? How is it recontextualised through these journeys?

> Holding half-drunk cups of coffee, Claire and Richard start walking in opposite directions out of City Academy's geography office, still discussing what to do with the boy who stole things from Claire's desk during a cover lesson and made moustaches from her post-it notes. The bell has rung, and the corridor is filling up with students bustling towards their next lesson. Footballs are mostly put away in bags, and lunchtime is over. Some queue quietly, gazing out the window; others push, and start play-fighting. Going to their separate classrooms, Richard and Claire are greeted with cries of 'Alright Sir', and 'Alright Miss'. 'Go in and sit down' they both call; Richard to his GCSE class, and Claire to her year sevens. The office doors close behind them, students file into classrooms and find seats; quiet reigns. Paul breathes a sigh of relief; free period! 'Right, what was I meant to be doing? Oh yeah, year nine tomorrow morning…' Claire and Richard are both in front of their classes, standing before them as geography teachers, and about to teach them. What knowledge are they seeking to teach to these students, in this school, this afternoon? Where did it come from? What is

DOI: 10.4324/9781003321682-5

> the nature and scope of this knowledge? Do Richard and Claire's choices relate to one another? And to Paul's; what will he teach to his year nine class?
> (Puttick, 2015, p. 14)

Information has always been moved by people, which in the scene above focuses on geography teachers searching and making selections about what information to introduce to these particular students at this time in this school. Information goes on journeys as stories and artefacts are taken, passed on, shared and re-told. One of the problems with a static, detached view of Africa such as the portrayal in *Prisoners of Geography* is that it imagines an Africa without connections or interacting communities. Communities isolated and cut off, unaware of the larger stories of the world that are being written and played out. But this myth is merely that: a myth constructed against the vision of a hyper-real Europe of global interconnections. Returning to Vasco Da Gama, his journey up the East coast of Africa illustrates these circulations of information and its geographical journeys well. Just as the ocean water flows around the Cape and the winds track across the seas, so too information is flowing around their journey. There is no internet, but messages are communicated, and intrigue is sparked. Who is the Gujarati navigator they final in Malinde and employ to take them across the Indian Ocean? What stories does he bring from Gujarat, and what information – about waypoints, currents, stars and winds – does he embody? When they arrive at many of the ports along the coast, their journals note that the communities have already been told information about them. They are expecting Da Gama's arrival and have been equipped with intelligence, normally about their conduct and religion. Warnings to heed, or encouragements to engage; information that tells something of interest about these ships and the people on them. These communities are interconnected, and communication channels (and other connections, including trade) exist between them.

One key movement of information that is often hidden in the accounts of European explorers is the transfer of information between them and local peoples. In particular, in the direction of flows of information, knowledge and expertise from local people to the Europeans. Throughout accounts of European expeditions to Africa and Asia, there is a deep reliance on local knowledge and information for navigation. For example, Stanley (1875–1876, p. 135) describes how it was 'by questioning natives' that they came to know their location (by that point at the western side of Wahumba). They hired guides in Ugogo, but these guides deserted Stanley at Muhalala, where he hires more. Guided by these locals for a further day-long march north-west, they also desert Stanley in the night. He describes waking to find himself 'left on the edge of a wide wilderness without a single pioneer'. After becoming lost in a 'labyrinth of elephant and rhinoceros trails', Stanley sent out 'the best men' to find their track:

> But they were all unsuccessful, and we had no resource left by the compass. The next day brought us into a dense jungle of acacia and euphorbia, through

> which we had literally to push our way by scrambling and crawling along the ground under natural tunnels of embracing shrubbery, cutting the convolvuli and creepers, thrusting aside stout, thorny bushes, and by various detours taking advantage of every slight opening the jungle afforded...One the evening of the third day the first death in this dismal waste occurred....
> (p. 135)

Without local expertise, the consequences are felt swiftly and fatally. Having the right kind of accurate information in this context is literally life and death. Broader arguments about the production of social science knowledge and the extractive processes this has been tied up with point to the ways in which the journeys of this information have involved hidden and harmed peoples.[1]

Mountains, information and hidden people

Mountains have functioned as an amazing backdrop to many geographical adventures. There is a romantic allure to the mountains in which 'rugged individualism went hand-in-hand with rugged aesthetics...the higher, the more remote, the more rugged, and the more sublime, the better' (Simpson, 2018, p. 562). Mountains are also symbols that played a key role in forming British national and imperial identities. In his account of *British Mountaineering on the Frontiers of Europe and the Empire, 1968–1914*, Hansen (1996) cites H. B. George's 'fear' that if the Caucasus are part of Europe, then they are also now the highest mountains on the continent. No longer is Mont Blanc the highest mountain in Europe at 4,807 m; instead, Elbrus takes this mantle at 5,642 m.[2] George was a history tutor and Fellow of New College, Oxford, and founder of the Oxford Alpine Club. George's geographical imagination is tied up with visions of Empire, full of natural markers and political signifiers: 'We are well aware [writes George] how potent an instrument a natural boundary can be made in imperial hands' (p. 48). Elbrus surpassing Mont Blanc as Europe's highest mountain is a fear to George because of the lack of attention Elbrus has been given by British mountaineers: 'The Alpine Club must confess it to be rather discreditable that a country so admirably suited for the playground of Englishmen should have received so little attention' (p. 48). Lying at the frontier of the 'white' races, the racialised construction of these geographies is tied into how the country is pictured, and who it is 'for': a playground of Englishmen. Or in the barrister Comyns Tucker's terms, 'The Caucasus is too glorious a country...to be left to the savage races who, as a rule, are its only inhabitants, or to the Russians, who cannot understand its beauties' (p. 51). Blending metaphors from sport and imperialism, Hansen describes this as representing 'mountaineering as not merely a recreation, but part of the cultural re-creation of Britain as an imperial nation' (p. 48). In the case of the Caucasus, the boundary between cultures shifts from being between Europe and Asia, to in the minds of British mountaineers as it being a frontier between Britain and Russia. Further East, and imposing Britain into the

Indian sub-continent, Lord Curzon, Viceroy of India from 1898 to 1905, imagines the Himalaya as a frontier between Britain and Asia. Curzon was a strong supporter of proposals for British expeditions to climb Mount Everest. He imagined these expeditions as a part of the PR of Empire: a means of generating spectacle, front-page headlines and asserting dominance. Not having put a British man on top of Everest is therefore seen as a 'reproach', and so Curzon writes that

> I have always regarded it as rather a reproach that having the tallest, and in all probability, the second or third tallest mountains in the world on the borders of British Protected or Feudatory territory, we have for the last 20 year equipped no scientific expedition and done practically nothing to explore them.
> (Hansen, 1996, p. 61)

Hansen goes on to ask why Curzon found it a 'reproach', and George 'discreditable' that British mountaineers had not conquered the Himalayas or the Caucasus?

> These mountains represented a challenge to British climbers, and not merely because they were there as geographical features of the landscape. As boundaries, these mountains posed a challenge because of the specific cultural associations that British climbers used to distinguish the places they thought of as here, from the places they thought of as there. Mountaineers drew boundaries between Europe and Asia, between Asia and Africa, between India and Russia and China, between themselves and guides or porters or coolies, between the heights on which man had trodden and those to which he still aspired. Each of these divisions established a bond, not a boundary, between the climbers' personal identity and their imagined sense of Britain's racial, national, and imperial identities.
> (p. 65)

The experiences of British mountaineers between the 1860s to the First World War, and the ways in which they describe and write about these experiences, echo the discourses of discovery, exploration and adventure that the RGS and other explorers employed to speak about their journeys to the Arctic and Africa. Wild frontiers without civilization and in need of conquering by the British. There is an important sense in which mountaineering went on to play a formative role in the shaping of geography, and the ideas about height interestingly reflect parallel questions about knowledge and vantage points:

> [T]he uplands, and in particular high peaks, have often promised unparalleled fields of sight affording unique opportunities for knowledge gathering and spatial mastery. Yet they could also pose unusually strong impediments to sight, in the form of clouds, steep valleys, and perplexing topographies, as well as threatening vision's sensory primacy through demanding an unusual degree of embodied labour.
> (Simpson, 2018, p. 656)

In contrast – it is implied – the everyday lowlands offer only restricted fields of sight, with the correlation that any opportunities for knowledge gathering are weak: rather than spatial mastery, the restrictions of lowland views lead only to partial understandings of space. These contrasts are echoed in discussions around powerful knowledge through the ways that *powerful* and *everyday* are seen to represent either higher, more objective views (powerful knowledge) or lower, more subjective views (everyday knowledge). Examples of the kinds of knowledge produced in the mountains help to challenge this dichotomy because of the ways in which everyday indigenous knowledgesplay a central role in the creation of what has been assumed to be 'objective' European science. In his account tracing some of the previously untold stories about the ways in which knowledge was produced in the Himalaya, Fleetwood (2022) unpicks the naming, measuring, collecting and analysis to tell a more complex story about the reliance by colonial explorers on local knowledges:

> A central premise of this book [Science on the Roof of the World] is that the methods for surviving in these mountain environments mirrored the methods for making knowledge about them. Attempts by European surveyors and naturalists to address the scientific, political and imaginative coherence of the Himalaya in the first half of the nineteenth century is particularly reflected in the reconfiguration of practices and theories.
>
> (p. 2)

Instead of focusing on the European heroes, his emphasis is placed on the ways in which we might pay attention to the Himalayan people who guided, carried, brokered and translated, which acts to

> demonstrate the overwhelming extent to which measuring the mountains depended on pre-existing local routes, expertise and labour. Even while ostensibly exploring the mountains, surveyors were almost never stepping off paths that had existed for millenia prior to their scientific interest.
>
> (p. 3)

This approach contrasts with the more widespread portrayal of European explorers which often hides the other people involved in their journeys and investigations. A Turner painting – *Snowy Range from Tyne or Marma*[3] – illustrates the romanticised, mythologised view of European Himalayan explorers.[4] Centred in the foreground of the image is the only standing figure: a European man with a telescope to his eye, gazing across the Himalayan mountain range. Dressed in smart white trousers, tailcoat jacket and hat, his dress, stance and technology contrasts against dozen Bhotiya porters who are shown lying or sitting on the floor, bare-footed and mostly bare-chested. As Fleetwood points out, they are 'depicted lounging about, neatly fitting the trope of the 'lazy native'. However, their presence ultimately reminds us that surveyors and naturalists were always dependent on the expertise and labour of Himalayan peoples in the mountains' (p. 4).

Part of Fleetwood's argument is for 'further decentring the spaces of science' (p. 5), which is about breaking down 'classic diffusionist models of the spread of scientific knowledge from Europe to colonial peripheries, [effecting] a reorientation to India-centred perspectives on scientific practice' (p. 6). The 'diffusionist' models of the spread of knowledge are similar to the accounts retold in stories about the origins of British geography: British knowledge and technological development which is then spread throughout the Empire. This vision is central to the Victorian Civilising Mission of Empire. Schools need to be built throughout the Empire to spread British values and knowledge that has been discovered in Britain. There is a centre (Britain, maybe Europe) and a periphery (the rest).[5] Fleetwood outlines two main arguments against this core/periphery understanding of where knowledge is produced and in what direction the information flows: firstly, by arguing that there are other 'centres' which challenge the idea that there is only a single centre; and secondly by showing that those in the supposed centre are deeply engaged with and reliant on those who have been positioned as being outside the centre and only part of the periphery. This second argument is the one that we have followed above through a number of examples of European explorers to challenge the idea of them being lone individuals: Da Gama, Stanley and many others all relied on local information, knowledge and expertise to produce the geographical knowledge they went on to widely publicise (which is in addition to their reliance on this local knowledge for the more basic issue of staying alive). One example of the first argument – that many others outside of the British 'centre' were also generating new scientific knowledge[6] – is illustrated by the example of Raja Serfoji II of Tanjore which Nair (2005) describes as having developed a 'centre of calculation'. He uses the term 'centre of calculation' to echo the way that the English Enlightenment figure Joseph Banks has been referred to. We will also follow an aspect of this argument further in Chapter 6; *Where should we start from?* Interestingly, more recent work on Joseph Banks has also uncovered 'the diverse communities and agents with whom he engaged and upon whom he depended in the pursuit of imperial goals and natural history' (Werrett, 2019, p. 426): Echoes of the story repeated across these accounts of European explorers and scientists deconstructing the myth of the lone individual and instead painting a more complex picture in which information moves, is distributed, related to and constructed through interactions between diverse groups of people.

Online journeys of information

The increase in the availability and quantity of information between Victorian England and now is staggering. There are unprecedented quantities of information available to teachers and students, often through contested, digitally mediated online spaces.[7] To give one example of where information often comes from, focusing on the example of climate change education, we used a scoping review methodology to explore what we know about the sources of information about climate change that teachers were using.[8] The scoping review allowed us to identify and analyse over 600 papers, which were refined to 52 and then following further scrutiny there were 13 studies that addressed the question about the sources of information about climate change used by teachers. The attention given to countries in the Global North was striking, if inevitable: no attention was given in these studies to countries in the majority world. Nearly half of them – six – focused on just one country; the United States of America. These studies are limited by this spatial concentration, and also by the methodological approaches. All apart from two of the studies rely on teacher reports on the sources of information. All of the studies from after 2010 include four main types of sources: the internet; government sources; mass media; and professional development courses. There was one study we found asking these questions pre-2010, and in contrast they (Michail, Stamou, & Stamou, 2007) conclude that the internet is teachers' least used source of information about climate change. The rate of change of internet use and access is hard to comprehend. As recently as 2006, the global distribution of internet access was highly uneven (Roser, Ritchie, & O'rtiz-Ospina, 2015). Figure 1 illustrates this picture in which Europe, North America, Australia, New Zealand and Japan are among those countries in which over 50% of the population use the internet. Huge parts of the globe at this point have less than 10% of the population using

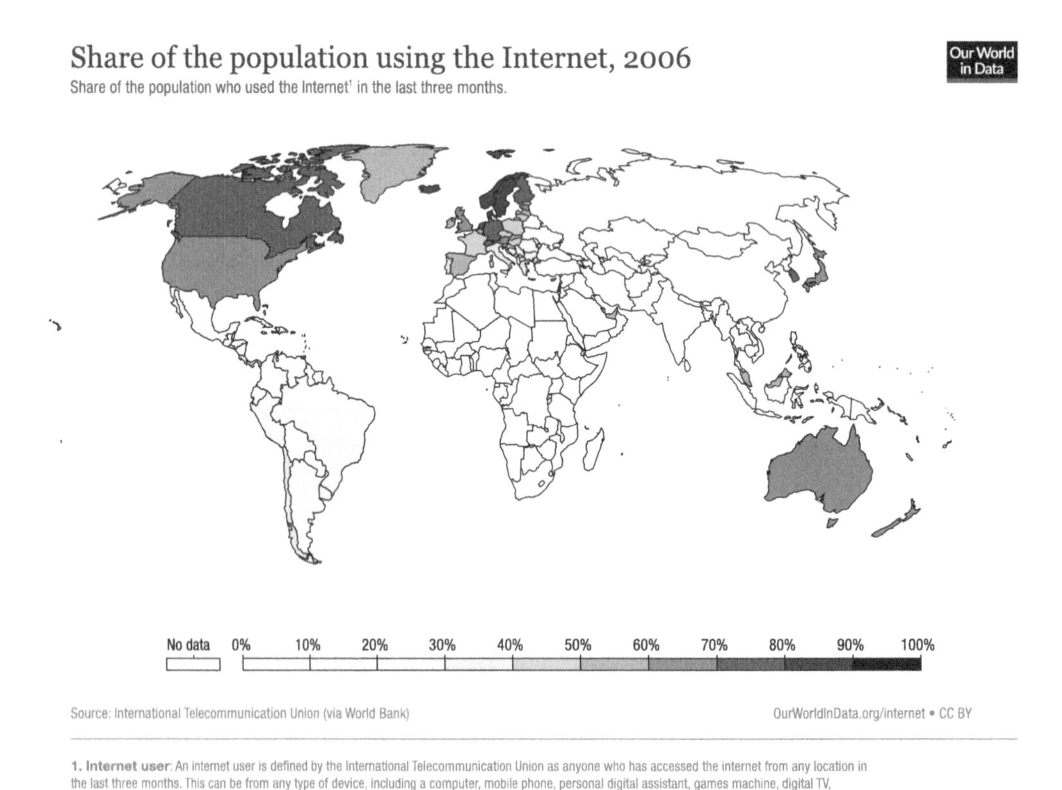

Figure 1 Share of the population using the Internet, 2006. https://ourworldindata.org/internet

the internet. Given the ubiquity of internet usage today this feels like a forgotten age. It seems almost unimaginable to have so much of the world not online at such a recent point in history.

Fast-forward 14 years and the picture shifts dramatically. The rapid rise in the share of the population using the internet is a global phenomenon. In many countries 80%, 90% and more of the population are using the internet. Yet this is still unevenly distributed. The shading across Africa and the Indian subcontinent in particular are, as percentages, noticeably lower (Figure 2). The uneven spread of internet usage is reflected in the kinds and locations of information that are made visible online.

To illustrate this issue about the poor representation in the types and representations of information that are made available online, I draw on the example of two Google searches that we conducted for the discussion of climate change education in the chapter *Climate Change Education: following the information* (Puttick et al., 2022). The work formed part of a larger project in collaboration between colleagues in Pune, India (Chopra, Singh and Chandrachud) and Oxford (Robson, Talks and me), funded by the Global Challenges Research Fund (GCRF): *Climate Change Education Futures in India.* The project asked questions about teachers' beliefs about climate change, with a particular focus on the kinds of information they use. We received over 500 full responses to the survey that we sent out, from which

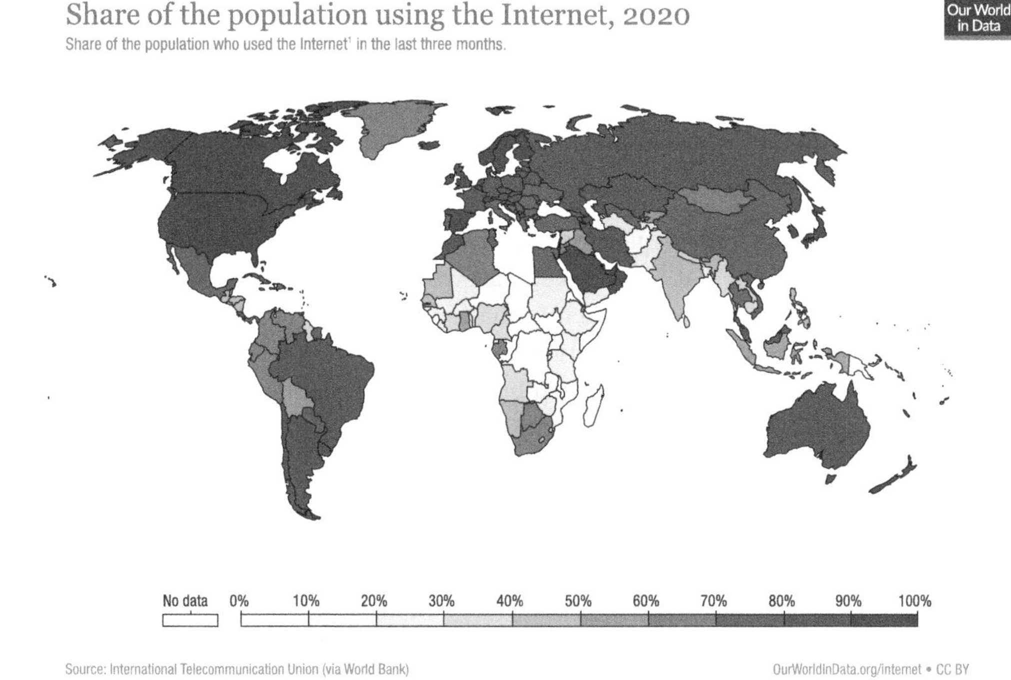

Figure 2 Share of the population using the internet, 2020. https://ourworldindata.org/internet

we conducted in-depth interviews with 48 teachers. This was a purposive sample that we chose from the survey respondents to include a range across; states,[9] subjects taught,[10] phases of education and gender. Given the diversity of these teachers, the similarity in their ideas about climate change is striking. There is a shared strong belief in the importance and centrality of climate change for education: 'it is the need of the hour' (Tanirika). This framing calls for climate change to be at the heart of the purposes of education, placing a weighty and emotional demand on teachers:

> [T]his has to be a continuous effort, a breathless action that has to be performed and I do it in this way, even if you ask any of children, even after 5 years they would say, yes definitely I have spoken to them about climate extensively and that brings out my emotion for them. I was filled with emotion because it was the need of the time.
>
> (Malika)

Or in another description, the urgency and obligation for action, and the scale of potential consequences are expressed by equating the changing climate as being 'like a bomb':

> Because if I say that there is a burning of these fossils and permafrost is thawing, we will talk about it like it is a bomb that is hidden at the moment and can explode any time. But how that incremental change in temperature every year is going to trigger that and then it will release carbon dioxide, methane into the atmosphere whose effects would be catastrophic. Can't even imagine how much impact it will cause and what will happen to the life on earth.
>
> (Vamil)

These teachers raised many questions about where information about climate change comes from, where it is produced and where it is about. They highlighted both the ubiquity of the internet as an information source, and the Anglo-American dominance of this knowledge production. For example, in describing the way that YouTube videos are 'interesting to watch but only the thing that they are referring to developed countries like America. They need to give more knowledge about the Indian scenario' (Tanirika). These absences of locally relevant and locally specific materials also relate to languages in the relative absence of materials they could access in languages other than English:

> You have more articles in the global scenario than in the local scenario. We really need to produce more article, or at least I'm not much aware of articles which are available in Tamil...it's actually a challenge to find in the local scenarios...
>
> (Sonali)

Hopefully, the broader context of the project gives some insight into these wider questions that we were exploring and into which we conducted this simple activity: one Google search carried out in Oxford, and at the same time, another Google search (using the same phrase: climate change primary school) carried out in Pune, India. The results from the search engine were fascinating. To begin with, the quantity of information made available, and which we see so frequently as to become blind to the scale of the numbers, is vast. The search in Pune returns 295,000,000 results in 0.42 seconds. Two hundred and ninety-five *million*! This is a huge number. If you were to count up to 295,000,000 taking just one second per number, you would be nearly ten years older when you had finished (and that is without stopping to sleep, eat, or do anything else). But all delivered in less than half a second. Most of the search results are not seen; normally, the first few hits and maybe the first page are viewed. The first ten results from these searches in Pune and Oxford have a great deal of overlap. Both begin with paid adverts for executive education courses in climate change; the Pune search saw a Cambridge advert, and the Oxford search showed an Oxford course. The search from Oxford not returning the Cambridge course seemed to be the only evidence of the geo-location of the searcher influencing the results that were returned. Both sets of results included, on their first page, a webpage from a single primary school in Doncaster. The first ten results from the same searches in Oxford and Pune both return exclusively Euro-American sources of information. The dominance of online searches of information for teaching raises critical questions about the geographies of knowledge production, circulation and consumption. For a world subject like geography, the absence of anything other than global north knowledge production brings implications for teaching, and new sites of challenge and resistance. This chapter concludes with a discussion that reframes contested online spaces and their digital geographies as new sites of exploration for geography teachers.

New journeys of information, old stories about statistics

How should teachers respond to these shifting patterns and shapes in the production, circulation and accessibility of information? What kinds of implications are there for young people, and what role should geography teaching play?

The scale and intensity in these rapid changes in information and knowledge systems or ecologies might also hide some of the similarities. There are enduring features of information and its journeys that have not changed. There has always been a need to critically evaluate things that you are told. Knowledge produced by people is always positioned in certain ways, in particular places, and it has always changed as it moves and interacts with other knowledges. Yes, quantity and speed have been dialled up to 11, but there are common processes that mean the geographical expertise that teachers have continues to be a key tool for understanding and engaging with the world. How might the patterns of internet usage, and the production of information and knowledge change in the future? And again, what role might – and should – geography teaching play in the evolution of these networked systems? What new journeys of information might geography teaching be a part of in our explorations of the world?

One response to these questions is to emphasise the last part of that final question: we are seeking to understand more about the world. In the next chapter (*Where should we start from?*), I make an argument for everyday exploration. This everyday exploration is about valuing the joy and wonder that comes from understanding the apparently familiar in new ways; peeling back layers of insight, changing perspective and appreciating the incredible in something we all too quickly assume to be merely mundane. So, there is tension between the former call to understand more about the world, and the latter encouragement to focus more on the local and everyday. Here, I am thinking about 'the world' mainly in terms of sources of information, drawing on arguments that have been made for worlding geography (Müller, 2021). In his analysis of the places in which geographical knowledge is produced (titled *Worlding geography: from linguistic privilege to decolonial anywheres*), Muller considers journal authorship, the make-up of editorial boards of journals, and major handbooks: elements chosen as proxies for where the power lies in geography for the roles they play in influencing and shaping the discipline of geography. The data leads him to make critical comments on the Anglo-American dominance of geography and to call for opening and expanding what counts and what gets included in geography. The idea of 'worlding geography' means 'opening up Geography, as a discipline with capital G, to those multiple unsung and untold places and voices that hide beyond the reach and grasp of current Geography and its privileged medium of English as a language' (p. 2). As an English speaker with only GCSE level German, I am obviously part of this picture, and as he argues, 'what makes this worlding difficult is the linguistic privilege that accrues from the dominance of English in geographical knowledge production' (p. 2). Not all knowledge is created, viewed or valued equally. The results from the Google search above offer one example, and also open one of the responses this is called for: actively and intentionally reading and citing work that is done in 'global anywheres' so that we are engaging with a multiplicity of knowledges.

These calls to engage critically, and to read and cite more widely are not necessarily new; there have always been voices in geography calling for more expansive engagement beyond a narrow cannon of accepted (white male) geographers. There have also been enduring questions about the role and relationships between the media and more scholarly academic geographies. But the medium is different, and there are new challenges in navigating and exploring these contested digital online spaces. Some of the questions and activities below offer some concrete suggestions for developing these kinds of critical journeys, resisting the dominance of certain platforms, searches and presentations of information. Before we get to them, I want to briefly focus on the media.

As a popular source of information for teaching geography is the media, it occupies a certain kind of space and reputation that gives it a privileged position. The media's status as a trusted, reliable (and impartial?) source of information is found not only across teachers in their accessing and sharing of media stories relevant to teaching, but also in the way that professional associations widely share media perspectives. As I write this, the Geographical Association's twitter feed yesterday included a link to a BBC (British Broadcasting Corporation) article on the impacts of climate change on flooding in the UK with the added text 'Climate Change: Warming to increase UK flood damage by 20% #geographyteacher'. Among media outlets, the BBC in particular continues to play an important (and contested) role in public discourse. Part of the contestation around the BBC is about culture wars, but amid some of the heated and polemical debate there are questions about impartiality and balance that have strong parallels with geography teaching. A recent review of BBC impartiality focused on the issues of taxation, public spending, government borrowing and debt (Blastland & Dilnot, 2022). This review offers a fascinating insight not only into the substantive issues Blastland and Dilnot were exploring, but also more generally into the challenges that come with the ideal of impartiality that teachers also often aspire to. Their methodology involved reviewing BBC output, documents, social media, and interviewing audiences, journalists and others. Overall, they found:

> Widespread appreciation for BBC coverage of tax, public spending, government borrowing and debt, and plenty to applaud. But against a test of broad impartiality, we also had concerns – about gaps and assumptions that put impartiality at risk.
>
> (p. 3)

The weaknesses that they identify mean that some output seems to lean more to the 'left' politically, while other examples lean to the 'right'. But 'curiously these lean left *and* right', and so they argue that they did not find evidence of systematic political bias. They did not find either leftwing or rightwing capture, from which they suggest that the weaknesses are not a political problem, but a journalistic one. To give one example, they think that

> [t]oo many journalists lack understanding of basic economics or lack confidence reporting it. This brings a high risk to impartiality. In the period of this review, it particularly affected debt. Some journalists seem to feel instinctively that debt is simply bad, full stop, and don't appear this can be contested and contestable.
>
> (p. 4)

Illustrating the way they found discussions about debt presented, they critically explore a chart shown on the BBC which cites the Office for National Statistics (ONS) as the source. On one level the chart looks like a simple, objective line graph. The ONS is highly reputable, and it merely states the UK public sector net debt in pounds sterling from 2000 to 2020 (p. 7). But, while 'none of the numbers here is wrong, exactly', they argue that it shows: a lack of understanding about the contestable nature of debt; the lack of information about the wider context (including whether the numbers are adjusted for inflation because if not then the rise will tend to be exaggerated, and the relationship with GDP); the use of £ (whereas economists would normally use percentage); and the time frame (what are the implications of showing the trend between those points when it is only rising? And as a contrast, they present an example stretching the frame from 1920 to 2020 which changes the picture to also include decades of substantial declines in debt as a % of GDP).

To give another example of their critique, the BBC website headlined 'UK debt now larger than size of whole economy' features a bar graph of 'borrowing by month over the past year': https://www.bbc.co.uk/news/business-53104734 The graph shows a number of blue bars, mostly above the zero line (that is, most show borrowing being increased). From April 2019 to the end of January 2020, the lines stay below £20bn. May's borrowing is then show significantly higher. Towering above, the colour is changed to red, with the amount also printed in red, bold text above that line. **May 2020: £55.2bn**.

The implicit message seems very clear: debt is bad, and this number is too high. The tall bars, even colouring in the biggest and most recent one red. Danger! Bigger than the whole economy sounds scary. Or maybe it doesn't when you take the example of household income and debt. Borrowing a mortgage to buy a house that is even 400% bigger than the whole of your annual income is very common and rather than feeling like a scary thing is widely believed to be a perfectly rational decision. Rhetoric framing Jeremy Corbyn's public spending proposals as needing a 'magic money tree' is one example of the way that the idea 'debt is bad' has been used in popular and political discourse. Blastland and Dilnot emphasise that their 'point is not to argue these views are definitive, or that debt is not a problem, or that more is right. It's to show why some people might reasonably think so. And some experts do think so' (p. 9). After critiquing the line graph showing increase in £ of debt, they emphasise the point: 'this does not mean we advocate going the other way and saying debt doesn't matter, or that a government has carte blanche. Its choices usually entail risks on all sides. We're saying there's serious argument, no more' (p. 13). These and other similar graphs are used in geography lessons (I suspect in a fairly widespread way, although I will limit my claim to the few times that I have personally been in lessons when they have been used!), and so Blastland and Dilnot's critiques, along with their suggestions for greater economic and statistical literacy in journalists, have some useful things to say for geography teaching as we think about the new journeys of information travelling into school geography classrooms.

There is a lot more about the use of data and statistics that we might say, including through the BBC impartiality report and Blastland and Dilnot's wider work

(For example, see: Blastland & Dilnot, 2008), and some of these themes are developed a little further in Chapter 7's discussions *What stories should we tell?* For now, I want to add just one further dimension to this discussion of critical engagement with media as a source of information for teaching geography: the potential benefits of focusing on accuracy. Both the Royal Society Report (2022) mentioned above, and Pennycook et al. (2021) find that people say that the accuracy of information is important, and that belief in disinformation and conspiracy theories is only held by a small minority (for example, the Royal Society report focuses on the examples of vaccines, 5G and COVID, and climate change). In Pennycook et al.'s work, they found a disconnect between widespread beliefs about the importance of only sharing accurate information, against the fact that inaccurate headlines are nevertheless widely shared. Offering suggestions for the ways in which social media platforms might use 'attention-based interventions' to counter misinformation online, they argue that 'subtly shifting attention to accuracy increases the quality of news that people subsequently share' (p. 590). There are implications for the kinds of questions that we might ask – and might encourage students to ask – of these vast and contested sources of information that are so readily and rapidly made available online.

Conclusions

Journeys of information are integral to the geography teaching adventure: where is this information coming from? Through what journeys does it travel into geography classrooms? Through what processes is it recontextualised, and what are the implications of these transformations? How can teachers and students make good decisions about what to include, where to search and how to present these sources? This chapter has opened up some of these questions by discussing findings from a range of different projects focused on the issue of climate change education, and in dialogue with Blastland and Dilnot's review of BBC impartiality. The role of mass media in teaching geography, and the function that 'newsworthiness' (Castree, 2014, p. 231) plays in shaping the kinds of questions and inquiries that are seen as legitimate, means that developing more critical engagement with the media is an important task. The importance of developing this engagement holds across the full breadth of geography, but is acutely felt in the case of socio-scientific issues of which climate change might be the archetype. As Castree puts it: 'never before has the news media covered a story about nature as grand in scale or profound in its implications as anthropogenic climate change. Its role as both gatekeeper and relay of others' claims stands to be hugely consequential' (p. 236). The incredible availability of information for geography teaching today – particularly online – presents amazing opportunities and brings a great deal of potential. Yet the way that age-old biases and privileges are baked into these online environments means that existing inequalities have been exacerbated rather than reduced through this potentially democratising force. The basic tension between the conflicting aims of making high-quality information readily available, and capturing users' attention to maximise advertising revenue, means that exploring online sources of information is neither simple nor value-free. The example of information on climate change for primary schools, through searches conducted in Pune and Oxford, illustrated the Anglo-American dominance of search result rankings and reinforced calls for more locally specific teaching resources. The next chapter *Where should we start from?* offers a response to these calls through a dual focus on worlding geography while also starting from the local and everyday.

Questions and activities

Where does the information that you present to students normally come from? Why do you choose those sources?

How do linguistic privilege and Anglo-American dominance impact geography knowledge production, and what steps can be taken to open up the discipline to a wider range of voices and perspectives?

How would you describe the ways in which information moves in today's world, and what impact does this have on the geography classroom? How have these patterns changed over your teaching career? How might patterns of internet usage and knowledge production change in the future? What implications do these changes have for young people, and what role should geography teaching play in this evolving landscape?

How can teachers use the geographies of information as a curricular resource and inspiration for further research and geographical inquiry?

What are the implications of the hidden and harmful journeys of geographical knowledge for geography education?

What challenges arise in navigating and exploring digital online spaces, and how can critical journeys be developed to resist the dominance of certain platforms, searches and presentations of information?

Choose and news story related to geography and critically evaluate it using multiple sources, including academic journals and online forums, news media outlets from multiple countries and social media accounts. How do these sources differ in their perspective, tone, positioning and analysis?

Choose a story on the BBC and analyse it in relation to Blastland and Dilnot's report on impartiality. What challenges does the idea of impartiality pose for media outlets? And what ways do debates about impartiality relate to geographical questions about information, data, representation, positionality and analysis of the world?

Research and map out the journey of a particular piece of information from its production circulation and movement into the classroom highlighting the geographical locations, connections, relationships, processes and actors involved.

Notes

1 https://theconversation.com/collaborative-indigenous-research-is-a-way-to-repair-the-legacy-of-harmful-research-practices-193912?

2 This replacement of Mont Blanc as the highest mountain in 'Europe' is particularly significant because of the symbolic role it had played as the yardstick by which others were compared. These comparative lenses were used so often that 'a 'Mont Blanc' came to be a de facto unit of measurement, and a scale to which all other heights were referred' (Fleetwood, 2022, p. 13). This role as defining norm also creates interesting moments when theories and understandings of mountains derived from these norms faltered when up against the far higher Himalayan mountains; moments which are 'reflective of the inherent unevenness of global comparisons, and who had access to what information and when', encouraging us to pay attention not only to 'circulation and connection in global history, but also disconnection, failure and resistance' (p. 14).

3 https://www.tate.org.uk/art/artworks/turner-snowy-range-from-tyne-or-marma-t05178

4 Also see the way Dodds Pennock (2022) flips this narrative, writing that 'this book is not about Montejo and Puertocarrero and their ilk, colonisers and conquistadors, white men striding out across the globe to appropriate it. This is the story of the people who travelled the other way…' (p. 1).

5 The centre-periphery model of global science has also been critiqued more widely for reproducing an inside/outside binary in ways that mirror previous North/South and West/East hierarchies. In developing an alternative approach to conceptualising the ways in which systems of scientific knowledge develop, Marginson and Xu argue for an 'ecology of knowledges' approach. For example, see: https://www.researchcghe.org/publications/working-paper/moving-beyond-centre-periphery-science-towards-an-ecology-of-knowledge/, and elsewhere for the centring of relational values at the heart of scientific knowledge systems (Yang, Marginson, & Xu, 2022). Throughout, this work raises important questions about how we understand and imagine the production of knowledge. Given the dominance of the centre-periphery model, and the reproduction of this through the stories told about the development of geographical thought, it is likely to permeate our thinking. Being aware of this, we might ask more critical questions about how we present geographical knowledge (such as; who we say discovered it, what characters we include in the story, how we portray the nature of the discovery as individual/collective/etc., where we centre, and so on).

6 Also see Eve Tuck's argument that 'since time immemorial, Indigenous communities have engaged in research activities, even when these approaches to research have been dismissed as unsystematic or not objective. Indigenous Peoples have always been researchers. Indeed, so many indigenous worldviews, knowledge systems and values are based in inquiry, curiosity and sharing the results of inquiry through storytelling'. Because of the collaborative nature of information produced, Tuck makes an argument for collaborative research that honours and respects indigenous knowledges: 'This approach is rooted in the belief that Indigenous communities have long pasts, and even longer futures. It begins with the premise that Indigenous people have expertise about their everyday lives and the institutions and policies that affect them. This expertise reveals how institutions and policies impede their hopes and dreams.' Tuck and colleagues' hope is that Collaborative Indigenous Research supports the 'agency and self-determination of Indigenous communities, often in collaboration with Black communities and communities that have also experienced colonial violence'. One practical solution Tuck has developed is the CIR (Collaborative Indigenous Research) Digital Garden; an openly available online space to learn, share and connect. At the time of writing it brings together over 200 studies.

7 For example, see the Royal Society report on the online information environment and misinformation online for a helpful summary of some aspects of the scale and contested nature of these spaces (Society, 2022).
8 https://www.bera.ac.uk/blog/climate-change-education-what-do-we-know-about-the-sources-of-information-teachers-are-using And for the full paper, see Puttick and Talks (2022).
9 Maharashtra, Tamil Nadu, Andhra Pradesh, Jammu and Kashmir, West Bengal, Punjab, Bihar, Jharkhand, Chattisgarh, Sikkim, Delhi, Madhya Pradesh, Uttar Pradesh.
10 Including geography, literature, physics, biology and mathematics.

References

Blastland, M., & Dilnot, A. (2008). *The Tiger That Isn't: Seeing Through a World of Numbers*. London: Profile Books.

Blastland, M., & Dilnot, A. (2022). *Review of the impartiality of BBC coverage of taxation, public spending, government borrowing and debt*. Retrieved from https://www.bbc.co.uk/aboutthebbc/documents/thematic-review-taxation-public-spending-govt-borrowing-debt.pdf

Castree, N. (2014). *Making Sense of Nature: Representation, Politics and Democracy*. Abingdon: Routledge.

Dodds Pennock, C. (2022). *On Savage Shores: How Indigenous Americans Discovered Europe*. London: Weidenfeld & Nicolson.

Fleetwood, L. (2022). *Science on the Roof of the World: Empire and the Remaking of the Himalaya*. Cambridge: Cambridge University Press.

Hansen, P. H. (1996). Vertical boundaries, national identities: British mountaineering on the frontiers of Europe and the empire, 1868–1914. *The Journal of Imperial and Commonwealth History, 24*(1), 48–71. doi:10.1080/03086539608582968

Michail, S., Stamou, A. G., & Stamou, G. P. (2007). Greek primary school teachers' understanding of current environmental issues: An exploration of their environmental knowledge and images of nature. *Science Education, 91*(2), 244–259. doi:10.1002/sce.20185

Müller, M. (2021). Worlding geography: From linguistic privilege to decolonial anywheres. *Progress in Human Geography*. doi:10.1177/0309132520979356

Nair, S. P. (2005). Native collecting and natural knowledge (1798–1832): Raja Serfoji II of Tanjore as 'centre of calculation'. *Journal of the Royal Asiatic Society, 15*(3), 279–302. doi:10.1017/s1356186305005298

Pennycook, G., Epstein, Z., Mosleh, M., Arechar, A. A., Eckles, D., & Rand, D. G. (2021). Shifting attention to accuracy can reduce misinformation online. *Nature, 592*(7855), 590–595. doi:10.1038/s41586-021-03344-2

Puttick, S. (2015). *Geography teachers' subject knowledge: An ethnographic study of three secondary school geography departments*. (DPhil). University of Oxford. Retrieved from https://ora.ox.ac.uk/objects/uuid:e83f4822-c40b-4217-b6b2-02a85da52b2a/files/m9fbaabc81ac05b48da46334aa0c6f4a0

Puttick, S., Chandrachud, P., Chopra, R., Robson, J., Singh, S., & Talks, I. (2022). Climate change education: Following the information. In J. McKendrick, M. Biddulph, S. Catling, & L. Hammond (Eds.), *Children, Education and Geography: Rethinking Intersections* (pp. 168–181). Abingdon: Routledge.

Puttick, S., & Talks, I. (2022). Teachers' sources of information about climate change: A scoping review. *The Curriculum Journal, 33*(3), 378–395. doi:10.1002/curj.136

Roser, M., Ritchie, H., & O'rtiz-Ospina, E. (2015). *Internet*. Retrieved from https://ourworldindata.org/internet

Royal Society. (2022). *The online information environment: Understanding how the internet shapes people's engagement with scientific information.* Retrieved from: https://royalsociety.org/-/media/policy/projects/online-information-environment/the-online-information-environment.pdf

Simpson, T. (2018). Modern mountains from the enlightenment to the anthropocene. *The Historical Journal, 62*(2), 553–581. doi:10.1017/s0018246x18000341

Stanley, H. M. (1875–1876). Letters of Mr. H. M. Stanely on his journey to Victoria Nyanza, and circumnavigation of the lake. *Proceedings of the Royal Geographical Society of London, 20*(2), 134–159.

Werrett, S. (2019). Introduction: Rethinking Joseph banks. *Notes and Records of the Royal Society of London, 73*(4), 425–429. doi:10.1098/rsnr.2018.0064

Yang, L., Marginson, S., & Xu, X. (2022). 'Thinking through the world': A tianxia heuristic for higher education. *Globalisation, Societies and Education*, 1–17. doi:10.1080/14767724.2022.2098696

6 Where should we start from?

Introduction

Where should we start from? This might sound like a silly question. Surely, we have no choice but to start from where we are. Wherever else we might want to start from, we are always already somewhere. Our journeys have to start from this where-we-are. People are finite and located somewhere. Despite even the greatest efforts of Victorian explorers to present their perspective as a God's eye view-from-nowhere, they like us all are people who think, write, teach and learn in particular places. One reason that I think this question (*where should we start from?*) is worth asking is that it can easily be ignored or skipped over. Like a free-flowing vantage point zooming across the (Google) Earth's surface, we might assume that we can actually start our adventure from anywhere. I will be thinking about where we start from in two different senses; one is about where our geography teaching might start from (and I will argue for starting with the local and everyday), and the other is about where our stories and understandings of geography as a subject and academic discipline start from. Whatever route we take, where a journey starts from, and where it leads to are related. In Tim Ingold's (2016) terms, there are *lines* joining them together. Or a web of different lines; most obviously the teacher and their students all beginning somewhere, and then going to somewhere else. Threads connecting metaphorical, material and imagined places together. This discussion follows from the exploration of information and its journeys to the classroom, which highlighted the Anglo-American dominance of knowledge production and representation, and offers some different (if paradoxical) ways forward that involve starting from the local and everyday, and also expanding our reading so that the geographies that we start from are part of worlding the subject and push beyond a narrow Anglo-American gaze.

My focus on reclaiming exploration therefore has a double implication for answering the question *where should we start from?* At one level, I think that reclaiming exploration means starting from where you are. Throughout this book, I have argued against an Orientalism that has infected school geography by creating a subject that is based in an environmental determinism to homogenise and rank peoples

DOI: 10.4324/9781003321682-6

and places and fetishize the exotic other. Against an obsession with faraway places, I have argued (and will do further in this chapter) for the importance of the local and everyday. At the same time, on another level, and thinking about the subject of geography itself, I want to do the opposite. Drawing on ideas about the Euro-American centrism of geography that were critically explored across the chapters to this point, I argue that we might reclaim exploration by pushing back against the Eurocentric dominance in the stories we tell about the subject. We might expand our understandings in a similar way to Radcliffe's (2017) argument that decolonial options move beyond a 'postcolonial provincializing of Western claims. Instead, the decolonial turn encourages re-thinking the world *from* Latin America, *from* Africa, *from* Indigenous places and *from* the marginalised academic in the global South…' (p. 329). Or in the specific example of Craggs and Neate's (2019) work: *What happens if we start from Nigeria?* In terms of geography as a school subject and an academic discipline, I am suggesting some rethinking of the characters we include, the shape of these narratives – and for the focus of this chapter – where we start from.

Starting from Europe

We tell massive stories about geography. We also tell massive stories through and with geography. They are so massive because in very few words we cover vast distances across space and time. In a single sentence we span the globe with our generalisations, charting the rise and fall of civilizations and characterising the hopes, desires, frustrations and successes of whole generations. Massive stories about whole megacities captured on half a page in a textbook. Many of the stories that have been told about geography as a school subject and academic discipline are similarly massive. This is not unique to geography, and in other accounts of how subjects have developed we see a similar pattern; a galloping across centuries of thought, debate, enquiry and exploration. Describing the philosophy of education, Oancea and Bridges (2009, p. 553) list influential philosophers whose ideas continue to be returned to; 'of Habermas and Heidegger, of Wittgenstein and Dewey, of Mill and Kant, of Hume and Locke and, to leap a few centuries, of Plato and Aristotle'. Leaping a few centuries. Where we start from is, in this sense, who we cite:

> Citation points to method and how we come to write what we know. Citation is important because it frames and supports (legitimizes) our argument. This also shows that if we begin with Michel Foucault as our primary methodological and theoretical frame – if Foucault is our referential scaffolding – we will, most certainly, draw Foucauldian conclusions. There is nothing at all wrong with a Foucauldian project and Foucauldian conclusions, of course – to suggest so would be remiss and skirt around the work of citations I am seeking to address. The example simply centralizes the importance of how referential beginnings and referential scaffoldings shape conclusions.
>
> (McKittrick, 2021b, pp. 22–23)

McKittrick sets the bar high, sketching a vision for deeply engaged intellectual work of research, teaching and scholarship. Ideas that might inform the way we see practical theorising, and here focusing on where we start from and the importance of explicitly acknowledging the others involved in producing the information and knowledge shared with students. 'When we are doing our very best work, we are acknowledging the shared and collaborative intellectual praxis that makes our research what it is' (p. 31).[1] This vision transforms a simple reference list into a dynamic, agentic force with shape, texture and direction. They lead us places, open new vistas and tell a story: 'reference notes are like map legends and cartographic keys that further explain how we read the plot, the cartogram, the borders, the diagrammatic data...' (p. 33). But who is included in these lists, and who is excluded?

Once upon a time, so the story goes, Greek philosophers wrestled with questions about time, space and other geographical issues. Once upon a time, Greco-Romans like Pliny the Younger wrote a Natural History *Naturalis Historia*, as geography's early work of naming, recording and categorising begins. Once upon a later time – leaping a few centuries – European explorers bravely 'did' geography. We map out Portuguese voyages of reconnaissance[2] showing the routes of Cao, Covilha, Dias and Da Gama. We praise Columbus for his geographical expertise and discoveries,[3] for how he was

> [p]ossessed of very considerable navigational skills and geographical awareness. His observations of various astronomical phenomena and his detailed knowledge of the wind circulation systems of the sea reveal his competence as a mariner; his profuse annotations on the margins of various contemporary geographical works, particularly the *Imago Mundi* and the travels of Marco Polo, demonstrate his scholarly commitments.
>
> (Livingstone, 1992, p. 45)

All of these Once upon a times are also Once in a space(s). Time-space is bound together (Massey, 2005), and our stories about geography start from the hyperreal Europe of Antiquity: a Greco-Roman fiction. Leaping a few centuries, they emerge blinking in the daylight of Empire-building expeditions. Starting with Europe means starting with fiction: a time-space that collapses time to intimately connect a Golden Age of Greco-Roman civilization with Enlightenment Rationalism. These stories betray misconceptions about geography, history and the history of geographical thought, misconceptions which are made particularly clear around the framing of the so- called 'Dark Ages'. In Walford's (2001) version of the story of geography, he argues that

> little [geographical education] survived as the 'Dark Ages' closed over Europe, as travel and exploration diminished and as the curriculum for the small minority who were educated in formal institutions became more narrowly

> circumscribed...The flame of wider geographical education in British Schools was relatively dim until interest was renewed by the discoveries of sixteenth and seventeenth centuries and by the beginnings of Empire.
>
> (p. 4)

This is a naïve and populist misunderstanding of the term 'Dark Ages'.[4] There is no space here to explore this term further, nor the representations of the whole period in this pejorative way, but the footnotes point to introductions of some of the highly sophisticated thinking developed in this period.

The misunderstanding of the Medieval world is a part of the colonial project's storytelling and myth-making about England, Europe and the rest of the world. It is vital that sophisticated advances made elsewhere much earlier are either ignored or repressed because unpicking these threads would unravel the whole fiction of England as 'naturally' occupying a 'higher' position in these ideological hierarchies that are used to rank civilizations. One of Walford's arguments that we examined above related to the kinds of experiences and beliefs that are attributed to people. In particular, he argues that comments about groups being seen as 'exotic' reveal 'how insular people generally were, how little they knew of each other and how far away the world was from being a 'global village' at this time...' (p. 22). Above, I focused on the defence that Walford offers for the homogenising descriptions of whole people groups, and I questioned the assumption that immediately removed any sense of responsibility from the geographical authors by appealing to the same environmental determinism that is so problematic in Mackinder's work: *they are just a product of their time.* The move to generalisations (*generally...*) is far too quick and unevidenced, and these stories about the past might be described as 'chronological snobbery' (Lewis, 1955).

Once upon a time-space, there were also other time-spaces; millions of lives being lived and (other) stories being written. What happens if we do not start from this hyperreal Europe, but instead start from elsewhere? What happens if we acknowledge and try to explore the ways in which geographical thought is and has been produced elsewhere? Rather than starting with Da Gama and praising his superior navigational skills, what if we start with the Gujarati navigator who had made the voyage from the Malabar Coast of India to the East Coast of Africa many times before (in the 1400s, with no GPS), and without whose expertise Da Gama would likely never have made it to India? Or what if, rather than starting with the later European world maps, we begin with the medieval Arab Muhammad al-Idrisi's *Tabula Rogeriana*?

Starting with al-Idrisi

The Tabula Rogeriana of Muhammad al-Idrisi – the world map shown in Figure 3 – was a remarkable achievement. This image constructed in the 1100s should be enough on its own to explode lazy myths about the 'dark ages'. To consider this map is to start in another space, to start in another time-space. There is so much the map can tell us and so many questions that it stimulates. The image shown in Figure 3 has been put together from the multiple map books that al-Idrisi created. If you

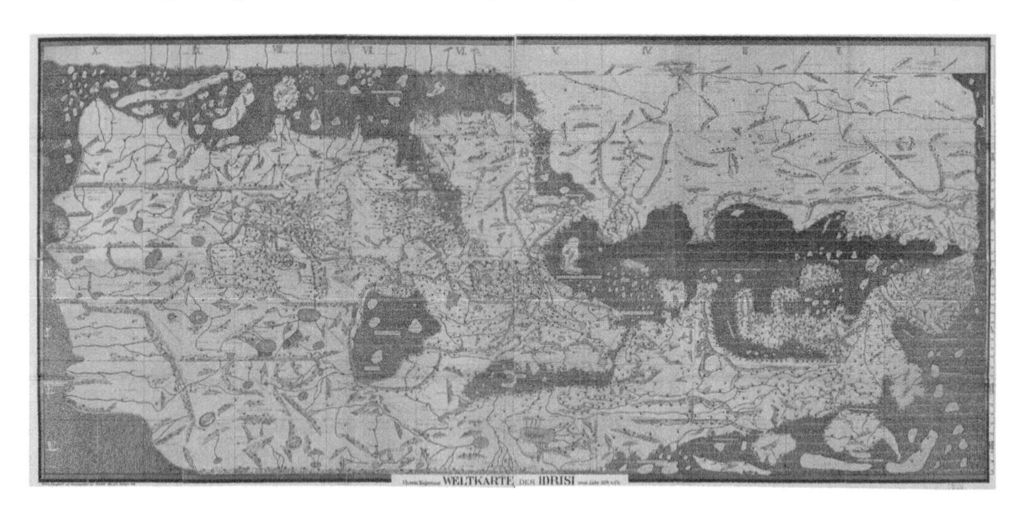

Figure 3 Weltkarte des Idrisi vom Jahr 1154 n. Ch., Charta Rogeriana. Library of Congress, Geography and Map Division: https://www.loc.gov/resource/g3200.ct001903/

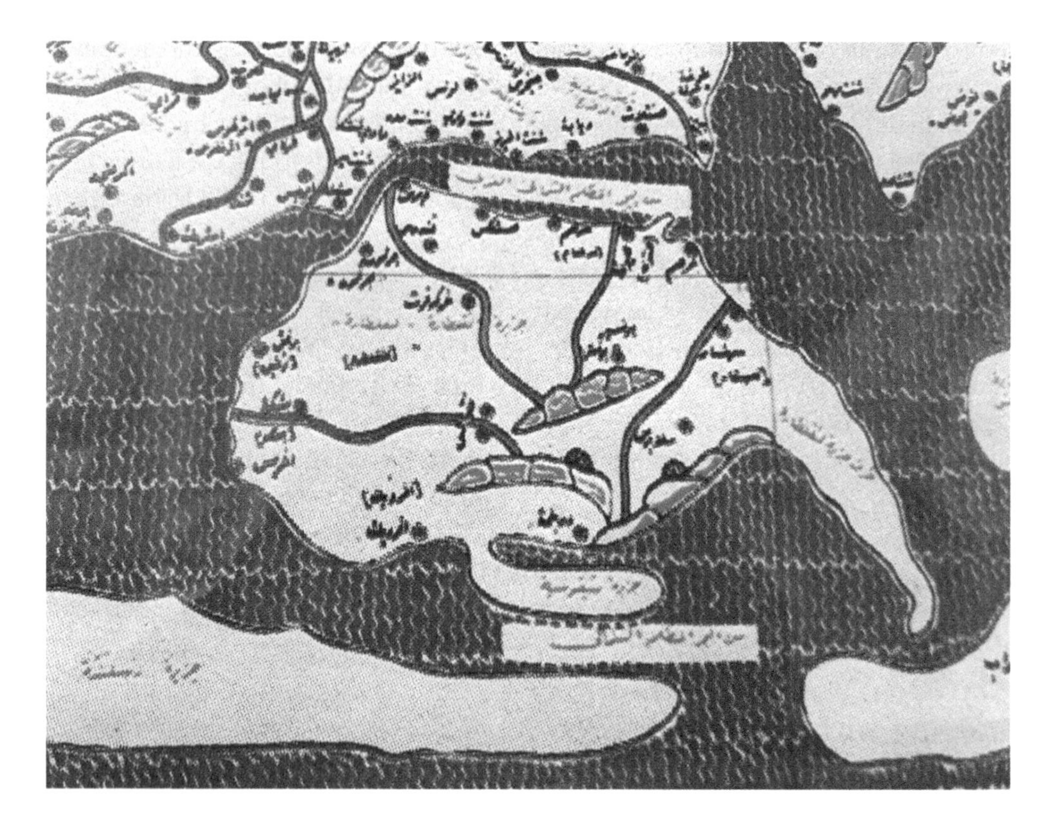

Figure 4 Detail of Britain from al-Idrisi's world map (Author's photograph of Bodleian library copy)

look closely, you will see the northings and eastings (the vertical and horizontal grid lines) are slightly staggered in places where these different sections have been connected. Muhammad al-Idrisi was born in 1100 in Morocco, and lived until 1165 or 1166. A ground-breaking geographer, al-Idrisi wrote what is largely regarded as one of the great works of medieval geography: *Kitāb nuzhat al-mushtāq fī ikhtirāq al-āfāq* (The Excursion of One Who is Eager to Traverse the Regions of the World: Muhammad al-Idrisi, 1154).[5] Al-Idrisi spent part of his life in the service of Roger II, the Norman King of Sicily, who commissioned him to create a world map on a large solid silver planisphere to be displayed in his court.[6] The breadth of detail on the map is staggering, with the information gathered from first-hand experiences and his conversations with Arab, Greek, African, Asian and more travellers, traders and explorers. This Arab geographer is not a mere side-note to the 'real' geographical tradition following a Greco-Roman myth. The South-top orientation of the map, and the relative position of England on this representation is also striking in the way it pushes home the message: what if we don't start from England? Can you find England on the map?

It is located in the bottom right-hand corner, shaped a little like an upside-down teapot.[7]

One thing that strikes me about the map is the deeply interconnected, networked world that it shows. There are vast numbers of settlements, and you can almost imagine the journeys, trading and communicating. The places, the Arabic script labelling names and those connections between places create a buzz; there is a vibrancy and productivity. The Iberian peninsula (right-hand side of the map) touches the African coastline, and the brown dots the whole way along the coastline of Africa indicate the frequency of these towns and trading ports. We reach the Nile (moving to the left across this coastline) and trace the river inland with dense pockets of inhabitation along it. Further East (continuing left on this projection) and we reach the Persian Gulf, Sri Lanka and India. Settlements in Southeast Asia are labelled, with trade routes and connections clearly shown. This is no 'dark age' with reductions in travel and communication. It just depends where you look and what you 'see'. Where you look from affects what it looks like, and to think back to the call for practical theorising introduced at the start of this book, the kind of exciting, challenging, adventurous intellectual work this demands is about starting from a wider view of geography and one in which the relationship between citation practices (whose voices contribute to the story) and theory (including how the subject is conceptualised) are critically and explicitly opened for discussion and reflection. Making choices about *where you start from* is to already engage with doing theoretical work. Who you speak to, and whose knowledges contribute to the geography shapes the very nature of the subject. As many have now argued, 'geography has failed to accommodate 'indigenous ways of knowing'' (Eaves, 2020, p. 34), and in Eaves' argument this is not accidental but is tied up with reinforcing and deeply embedded power relations. It takes effort to think otherwise and to build what she refers to as 'an other geography'. Al-idris's world map is one example of the kind of counter-narratives that might be told to reclaim exploration and inspire richer and more complex stories about geography and about the world.

Starting from the Global South

The terms we use to refer to regions are contested and contestable. The identifier 'Global South' is not exempt from this and has received criticism, including for the way in which it over-generalises. I am using it here following Hedding and Breetzke's (2021) arguments in their paper *"Here be dragons!" The gross under-representation of the Global South on editorial boards in Geography*. As the title suggests, their argument supports Müller's (2021) prompts for worlding geography discussed above. It is an extreme situation; the under-representation is *gross*. Hedding and Breetzke focus specifically on the make-up of editorial boards by analysing 126 geography journals, which includes 5,202 editorial board members. They found that almost 80% of these editorial board members are located in mainland Europe, North America and the British Isles. In contrast, Central America, South America, the Middle East and Africa combined contain just 5% of these editorial board members, and in addition to this, these editorial board members we concentrated in the 'lowest quartile' journals as judged by impact factor (which, although it is a silly measure and a poor proxy for the 'quality' of research, nevertheless continues to be an influential marker of prestige in academic geography). They argue that these findings about the Euro-American dominance of editorial boards 'highlight the outdated and exclusionary practices that pervade the scholarly publication process in science in general, and Geography specifically' (p. 331). Editorial boards play a key role as gatekeepers of disciplines, setting the direction or trajectory of the subject and deciding what kinds of knowledge are accepted as legitimate. What should be published, and what kinds of questions should be pursued? These arguments for worlding geography are about making it a little more transparent that our geography has often started from a particular kind of place, and these places bring certain racialised, classed and gendered kinds of privilege and exclusion. They shape what we 'see', and so calls for worlding geography are about expanding, shifting and diversifying our vision: what happens if we start from the Global South? What views are suddenly brought into sharp relief? What can we then 'see'? In one fascinating example of following this kind of approach, Craggs and Neate (2019) pose the question: *What happens if we start from Nigeria?* Flipping the starting point of geography itself from an assumption that we start from British (or at most, Euro-American) geography, this account opens opportunities to re-tell stories about geography not only as a Eurocentric endeavour in which the 'natural curiosity' is then immediately associated with 'natural' European origins, as opposed to 'un-natural', 'un-curious' others: assumptions that immediately bring associations with different ideas about race, hierarchies and levels of civilisation, productivity and development. Instead, this re-telling is to understand geography as a global endeavour that has been engaged with interestingly in multiple places and times. Against Walford's 'starting from Europe' that claims that 'we' know little of 'other' geographies, this is a call to widen the stories about the development of geography in ways that actively engage with 'worlding' (Müller, 2021) the subject.

The subtitle of Craggs and Neate's paper is *Diversifying Histories of Geography.* By analysing archival evidence, and conducting oral history interviews, they frame this 'starting from Nigeria' as offering new perspectives that 'highlights the intellectual contribution of Nigerian scholars, illustrating the partial and exclusionary nature of many traditional histories' (p. 899). They track the movement of Nigerian geographers, many of whom gained postgraduate geography degrees in London, and then returned to University College Ibadan (which after 1962 was University of Ibadan), the first university in Nigeria. Through the stories of these individuals and communities, Craggs and Neate are

> as interested in friendships, solidarities, disappointments, and exclusions as in publications. It is in this wider understanding of academic labor that it is possible to better understand the experience, opportunities, and challenges of university careers developed against the backdrop of decolonization and ongoing coloniality.
>
> (p. 901)

In starting with Nigeria, they foreground the work of Mabogunje,[8] and argue that he and his colleagues 'are not a central part, or even a footnote, in many histories of geography that claim universality while consistently prioritizing work in the West' (p. 912). Healy and colleagues' work in Bolivia is also framed in this way,[9] as starting *from* Bolivia and Peru, which they describe as focusing on understanding sustainable development in a way that starts from and is situated within the countries. Central to the development of these understandings, research and teaching resources are the intellectual contributions of Indigenous leaders and communities. The point is that 'this debate must include voices, ideas, scholarship, and places in the world that have been under-represented in geography's publication venues over the years' (Daley et al., 2017, p. 3).

Starting from the local and everyday

The first response above to the question *where should we start from?* was about starting from global majority geographies, which for those coming from Eurocentric perspectives is about going further and drawing on a far wider range of voices and sources of information; expanding the focus of enquiry. Somewhat paradoxically, I now want to argue that reclaiming exploration might also (both/and, at the same time) offer a quite different response. Instead of looking to far-flung exotic others as the source of geographical inspiration and adventure, we might begin much closer to home starting from the local and everyday. This is about flipping the starting point of our exploration so that in contrast to Walford's conception that sees geography as firstly about 'other' distant places, we instead begin by focusing on critical explorations of 'our' local places.

At a time when global travel is easier and cheaper than at any previous point in history, it might seem counter-intuitive for this chapter to centre the importance of local, everyday places. In this chapter the adventures of geographical exploration are reimagined from idealising the distant and exotic, to instead valuing the local every- and any-where. The aim of the chapter is to persuade that it is not just through seeing new distant vistas that wonder might be experienced and new stories told. Rather, geographical insights might enable us to see the local and everyday anew, and from this basis re-consider the ways in which other local and everyday places might be engaged with through global connections and travels. In part, this is inspired by Indigenous ways of knowing and educating that honour our connections to place. For example, these ideals are foregrounded in the way that Huaman (2022) explores *How Indigenous Scholarship Changes the Field: Pluriversal Appreciation, Decolonial Aspirations, and Comparative Indigenous Education.* An important aspect of their project is in centring Indigenous knowledges and self-determination. The strong place-based and place-accountable forms of education that emerge in their accounts of Indigenous work challenge the 'view from nowhere' assumptions about knowledge and teaching touched on above. There is a responsibility to the local and everyday that endows it with value, dignity and wonder, and these

> attachments to place – including new and made places – should not be confused with provincialism but that land, waters, winds and their beings flow and communicate with each other in very real ways that also influence how [Indigenous] education is currently responding.
>
> (p. 400)

Starting with the local and everyday is also a way to rethink how we understand other places: transforming them from being 'distant' and 'exotic' to instead firstly and most importantly being (someone else's) local and everyday. To illustrate the idea of starting from the local and everyday I will briefly explore some ideas around buildings, past climates, new perspectives and peeling back layers of experience and meaning through two places: Kolkata and Oxford.

Kolkata

The photos below were taken as part of a collaboration with Immersive Trails, funded by the GCRF. The aim of the project was to take some of Immersive Trails' approach towards local walking tours and make the process, and some specific examples, accessible and relevant to schools. Their approach involves rigorously researching areas through a combination of archival research, first-hand accounts, map work and reviewing the wider literature and research on the area. It is fundamentally about starting with the local and everyday (and interestingly it is not primarily tourists who use their walking tours, but local people keen to see their everyday from a new perspective). Immersive Trails describe their work as purpose-driven, seeking to make travel and learning more accessible and enriching by translating in-depth, ethical research into immersive experiences – in person and virtual. Tathagata Neogi and Chelsea McGill originally co-founded Heritage

Figure 5 Entrance to the Calcutta Art Studio (Photo Immersive Trails)

Walk Calcutta and have developed that expertise through Immersive Trails,[10] who believe that:

> Everyone has the right to travel, learn and experience unique stories from all corners of the world, irrespective of their financial or physical ability. We also believe that if you have an interesting story to tell about your backyard, you deserve to show it to the world. At Immersive Trails, we bridge these two aims by curating and helping others curate immersive in-person & virtual experiences which allows people from all over the world to have easy access to discover and learn.[11]

The basic aim of our collaboration was to facilitate teachers to see their local places in new ways; to re-tell stories that might otherwise be ignored or forgotten. In the specific example that I want to share here, stories which might otherwise simply be walked or driven over.

Calcutta Art Studio is a print house based in Kolkata that has been specialising in lithographic printing since 1878.[12] As part of the project, we were interested in exploring the interactions between the printing house, colonial Britain, traditions of print-making and the circulation of information and artefacts. Their extensive

Figure 6 Calcutta Art Studio; Print of the goddess of learning Maa Saraswati. Photograph Immersive Trails

back catalogue includes some auspicious Bengali artwork, such as the print of the goddess of learning, Maa Saraswati, shown in Figure 6.

There is a rich cultural history of production and circulation that the studio has played a key role in, and these stories and artefacts themselves offer some fascinating curricular resources. Here we were thinking particularly in the local and everyday context of teachers in Kolkata: opening ideas and information produced in a building they and their students might otherwise just walk past every day.

Figure 7 Parking area outside the Calcutta Art Studio. (Photo Immersive Trails)

Tathagata and Chelsea also noticed something else, and their observation offers a wonderful example of peeling back layers that local and everyday exploration might hold. Figure 7 looks out from the Calcutta Art Studio across the area they use to park cars and motorbikes (the photographs in Figures 5 and 7 look towards each other/where the other photo was taken from). The slabs are polished from the passage of feet and tyres. But what are those slabs? What were they made for? Probably functional construction tiles? Our Immersive Trails colleagues were not so sure. Why are they shaped like that? What stone are they made from? There was something intriguing and so they looked further. They asked if one might be removed from the floor and be lifted up. After a little persuasion (why would you want to do that?!), the tile was taken up, flipped over, and instantly the understanding of the tile and its purpose and function was transformed. Turning it over revealed the underside to have a hidden identity. It was an old lithographic printing tile containing the relief of an important piece of art. This tile had once been used to create prints of Maa Saraswati (Figure 7). The everyday parking surface contained – quite literally in this case – hidden stories, which I think brilliantly captures this notion of starting with the local and everyday. The buildings around us, and the ground beneath our feet all have stories to tell. Let's bring more of these stories into the classroom.

Oxford

Starting from the local and everyday, I felt that I had no choice but to include the example of Oxford as my local and everyday, and in this context I want to use ideas around past climates, building materials and new perspectives to offer a sense of some of the explorations that we might take students on. These local and everyday adventures are meant to be generative: to stimulate more exploration in this specific case and beyond.

Past climates

The ground beneath our feet has countless stories to tell. How many of them do we know? How many of them do we tell our students? In what ways might we make concepts and ideas come to life by connecting them with places, artefacts, buildings and landforms that they have seen and will continue to see almost every day? The Radcliffe Camera[13] (Figure 8) is home to part of the Bodleian library. Over half a million books and inside bear witness to wonders of accumulated wisdom, knowledge and insights. So too do the stones themselves have incredible stories to tell. The sun glinting off the oolitic limestone against a clear Spring Oxford sky makes the rock shine: 160 million-year-old limestone formed under tropical seas now quarried, shaped and revealed to view, each stone playing its role in the structure of James Gibbs' neo-classical masterpiece funded by the estate of John Radcliffe in the mid-1700s. The upper storey and columns are made from Taynton

Figure 8 The Radcliffe Camera, Oxford (Author's photograph)

Stone (approximately 166 million years old); the lower storey is made from Headington Freestone ashlar, and the lowest white plinth from Headington Hardstone, both approximately 160 million years old.[14]

One-sixty million-year-old fragments polished and shining at you. This is incredible! 160 million years old. Walking along, as the rock catches your eye, take a moment to get some perspective and breathe in the depth of geologic time. 160 *million* years. These kinds of limestones are formed under shallow tropical seas, and if you are standing where the photo was taken, then 160 million years ago that is exactly the kind of landscape that you would have found. A bit like the view shown in Figure 9 from a beach in Boracay.

Figure 9 Looking West from Punta Bunga Beach, Boracay, Philippines (Author's photograph)

Ooids that form part of these limestones are made from tiny fragments (such as fragments from shells) which become laminated, forming spherical (or similar) carbonate grains under 2 mm diameter, with this formation often happening in shallow, warm water and the kinds of conditions which today are found in the East Indian Archipelago (such as in Boracay shown above), and the Bahamas (Diaz & Eberli, 2019). Similarly, the stony corals that make up part of the Headington stone flourished in these same conditions. These corals rely on a symbiotic relationship with photosynthetic organisms, so they need light: shallow, clear warm water with optimal calcium carbonate production happening between 20 and 25°C. Today, these conditions are typically found between 30°N and 30°S: the topics. But Oxford is not in the tropics, and nor was it that far south in the Jurassic period. The geological story that these stones speak of takes us into deep time and radically changing climates. Transforming how we imagine the streets we walk through and imagining these places otherwise, which in this example might involve using some of Arkell's (1935) research and mapping of coral reefs in the vicinity of Oxford.

Imagining these climatic, geologic and landscape changes – Coral Reefs around Oxford! – and doing so by delving into deep time, and then layering on top of this the construction of the Radcliffe Camera and these glinting limestone walls reveal new perspectives. It is not just sunlight sparkling from the hewn faces of the

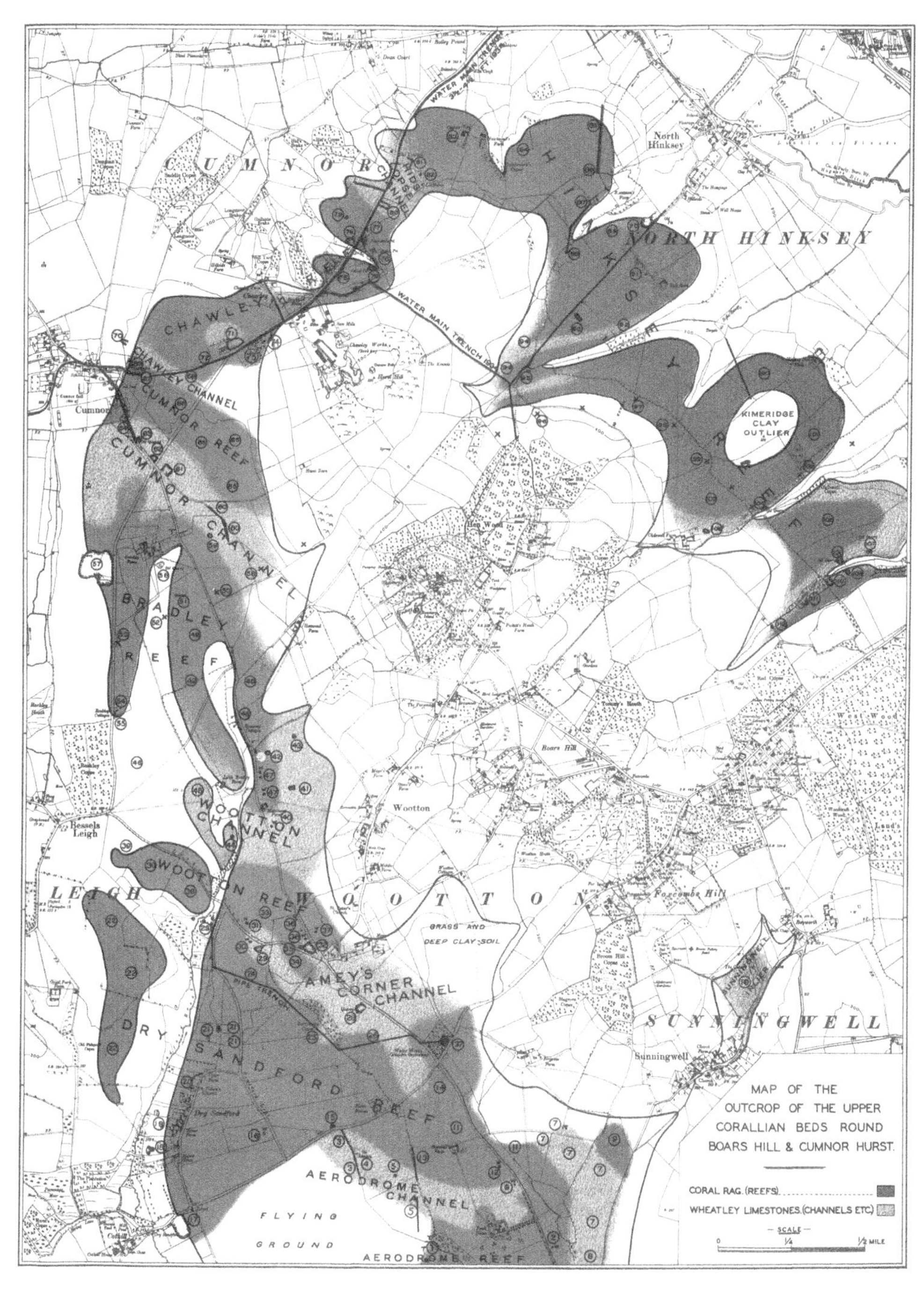

Figure 10 Plate VI Map of the outcrop of the Upper Corallian beds round Boars Hill and Cumnor Hurst, Arkell (1935, p. 111)

building. Shifting landscapes, climates and glimpses into the vastness of geologic time are also on view if you know where to look.

We might also see the local and everyday from a new perspective by more literally and physically changing the view: geographical explorations involving us moving around the area and engaging with local fieldwork. Just ten minutes from the centre of Oxford – and much closer than a three-hour coach journey to classic coastal fieldwork venues – is an incredible woodland: Wytham Woods. Going up to Wytham gives a panoramic view across the city. Taking students from local schools to the hill, you can look over the city and see the location of their school but from a new perspective.

Where we travel, and where we hold up as the ideal sites for geographical enquiry also have environmental consequences which are relevant to these arguments about reclaiming exploration. The unequal impacts of climate change raise questions about the carbon footprints of school field trips, particularly when these arguments are made in the broader context of colonialism and a pushing back against extractive forms of geography that leave the places visited in a worse state than we found them. Written from a discussion on academic conferences, Gossling and colleagues (2019) ask the question 'Can we fly less?' And as they put it, 'Aviation is increasingly in conflict with societal goals to limit climate change and challenges related to air pollution, noise and infrastructure expansion' (p. 1). Extractive

Figure 11 View from Wytham Woods looking East towards Oxford (Author's photograph)

geographies that result in expanding inequalities, unfair burden of impacts and risks are what this whole book is trying to critique, and fieldwork's contribution to this should be carefully considered.[15]

Conclusions

This chapter has posed questions about *where* we should start from and offered two slightly paradoxical responses. Narratives constructed about the geographical tradition have often hidden and erased Indigenous others, giving almost exclusive attention to the work of those in Euro-American contexts, and connecting them across space-times to an imagined 'true essence of geography' found in exceptionalism, Greco-Roman myths and 'doing' geography. This story has been told from particular places, often encouraging a geography that is about exotic, far-flung places. In these accounts of geography, geographical knowledge is produced 'locally' (that is, in Euro-American contexts), and it is about exotic others: the further away, the more different the culture and the more remote, the better. The first response that I developed is to invert this narrative and say that we should 'start' our geographical understandings and our searches for information with peoples and places that are far from Euro-American centres. It is an argument for constructing geographical knowledges in inclusive and expansive ways that benefit from the accumulated wisdom and insight of Indigenous and Black geographical thought. Who is on the reading list? What authors do you recommend? What authors are you reading? Where is portrayed in teaching resources? And where are these resources produced? How does the information flow and how might it change as it is recontextualised?

The second response was to argue (slightly paradoxically) that we should actually start from the local and everyday: the geographical experiences that we hold up as the *raison d'etre* of geography do not foreground long-haul destinations as the ideal type of geographical explorations. Through some brief examples in the contexts of Kolkata and Oxford, I illustrated some of the kinds of geographical exploration of the local and everyday that we might engage with, opening up stories about local geology, climate, industry and culture to help students rethink and re-enchant the local and everyday.

Thinking across these different examples, we are forced to shift scales. Geographical analysis is never static; it will not stay at the local and everyday, just as attention to the global is irresistibly drawn to specific local places. Connections, ecologies of knowledges and co-dependencies across institutions and disciplines are essential and so we shift between attention to the local and immediately think across scales, zooming out to global climatic shifts, travelling across millennia and ancient coral reefs. The exhibition *A Nice Cup of Tea?* (Figure 12) illustrates some of these points well.

The piece takes an everyday object (a teacup, saucer and teapot) and deconstructs them: exploding porcelain outwards from an imagined centre and provoking us to rethink this everyday object and practice. There is an almost 'unspeakable intensity that is animated by possibility' (McKittrick, 2021a, p. 15) as the piece

Figure 12 A Nice Cup of Tea? Art Installation, Ashmolean Museum (Author's photograph): https://www.ashmolean.org/event/nice-cup-of-tea

connects us across the Atlantic in one direction, and to tea growers in Asia in another direction. Raising critical and uncomfortable questions about colonialism, slavery and the logics of extraction, exploitation and inequality. Profound, urgent questions emerging from (firstly) re-exploring the local and everyday.

Questions and activities

Why is it important to consider where we start from when teaching geography? How can starting from the local and everyday challenge Orientalism and Eurocentrism in the subject of geography?

Reflect on the ways in which starting from the local and everyday can help you to appreciate the unique features and qualities of your community. How can this perspective inform your interactions with, and teaching about, other places and communities around the world? How might you connect these stories to other geographical concepts you are teaching about? How might you use them to inspire students to see their local and everyday in new ways?

What are some ways in which you can explore and learn more about your local area? Are there any walking tools museums or historical societies in your town or city that you can visit or make greater use of? How does exploring your local area help you to understand global issues and perspectives? Can you think of any examples of how your community has been affected by global events or trance? Research historical building or landmark in your local area. What is its history, and how has it been used over time? What stories and cultural traditions are associated with it, are there any opportunities for integrating these particular places, buildings and spaces to enrich the geography you are teaching young people about?

Collaborate with colleagues in the art department to create pieces of art inspired by the local area. How do these pieces reflect the unique features and characteristics of the community?

What geographers are you reading, or have played a significant role in your engagements with the subject? Map out their locations and look for patterns: what places dominate, and where is under-represented in your understandings of geography?

For any academic writing you might be doing, analyse the sources that you are using: where is the research 'starting from'? What are the implications of these starting points, and where else might you start from? How might you expand the places informing your research?

Notes

1 See also McKittrick (2006, 2021b), including further attention to the politics of citation.
2 For example, see Livingstone's (1992, p. 43) story of expeditions, sailors and how Portuguese efforts were then 'left to the indomitable Vasco Da Gama to all the way and stake Portugal's claim – now under Manuel I – in India. This he did in 1498 when on 22 May he touched the south-western coast of India, having displayed stunning navigational skills in his route around the Cape and across the Arabian Sea and the Indian Ocean'.
3 And this view is not restricted to Euro-American stories. For example, Zhishan (1993) argues that 'Christopher Columbus was indeed a zealous promoter, designer and great mariner…Whatever mishaps he met with before reaching new land, his daring initiative and original goal should already deserve the admiration of the Chinese people' (p. 178).
4 For a brief summary, see: https://time.com/5911003/middle-ages-myths/, and for an introduction to one example of the development of sophisticated scientific thought in Robert Grosseteste, see https://theconversation.com/our-latest-scientific-research-partner-was-a-medieval-bishop-42857 and https://theconversation.com/medieval-bishops-theory-resembles-modern-concept-of-multiple-universes-25460

5 For further discussion, see also Gaspar's (2018) discussion of the birth of Nautical Cartography, and Ferrer-Gallardo and Kramsch (2016) *Revisiting Al-Idrissi: The EU and the (Euro)Mediterranean Archipelago Frontier* who 'draw on the contemporary resonances of the destabilising cartographic imagination of Al-Idrissi (1100–1116)...the paper underlines the necessity of forging new vistas on the Mediterranean engendering perspectives that are more dialogical, plurivocal and sensitive to permanent transformation, as evoked by a long-standing spatial as well as political horizon of struggle' (p. 162).
6 For example, see: https://www.publicmedievalist.com/greatest-medieval-map/
7 How maps represent places shapes how we see these places and their relative importance. For a humorous explanation of this general point, see this West Wing clip Cartographers for Social Equality: https://www.youtube.com/watch?time_continue=226&v=OH1b-Z0F3zVU&feature=emb_logo
8 For example see: Mabogunje (2002) and Mabogunje (2004). A memorial on the AAG website to Mabogunje is available here: https://www.aag.org/memorial/akin-mabogunje/
9 See Healy et al. (2023).
10 For a broader discussion of local walking tours in dialogue with Uncomfortable Oxford, see the recording of the 'Live Stream with Heritage Walk Calcutta' here: https://www.uncomfortableoxford.co.uk/panel-discussions
11 https://www.immersivetrails.com
12 http://calcuttaartstudio.com
13 https://www.bodleian.ox.ac.uk/libraries/radcliffe-camera
14 For further information on Oxfordshire building stone, see: https://www.wildoxfordshire.org.uk/wp-content/uploads/2018/10/Oxfordshire_Building_Stone_Atlas.pdf
15 For example, see the recent discussion in the *Journal of Geography in Higher Education* exploring the paradox of the 'sustainable fieldtrip' (Telford, Valentine, & Godby, 2023). The views of the undergraduate geographers in their sample argue for greater use of virtual fieldwork and integrated approaches to reduce the carbon footprint of the activity, while also recognising the irreplaceability of being physically present in field sites.

References

Arkell, W. J. (1935). On the nature, origin, and climatic significance of the coral reefs in the vicinity of Oxford. *Quarterly Journal of the Geological Society, 91*, 77–110.

Craggs, R., & Neate, H. (2019). What happens if we start from Nigeria? Diversifying histories of geography. *Annals of the American Association of Geographers, 110*(3), 899–916. doi:10.1080/24694452.2019.1631748

Daley, P., McCann, E., Mountz, A., & Painter, J. (2017). Re-imagining politics & space: Why here, why now? *Environment and Planning C: Politics and Space,* 35(1), 3–5.

Diaz, M. R., & Eberli, G. P. (2019). Decoding the mechanism of formation in marine ooids: A review. *Earth-Science Reviews, 190*, 536–556. doi:10.1016/j.earscirev.2018.12.016

Eaves, L. T. (2020). Fear of an other geography. *Dialogues in Human Geography, 10*(1), 34–36.

Ferrer-Gallardo, X., & Kramsch, O. T. (2016). Revisiting Al-Idrissi: The Eu and the (Euro) Mediterranean Archipelago Frontier. *Tijdschrift Voor Economische en Sociale Geografie, 107*(2), 162–176. doi:10.1111/tesg.12177

Gaspar, J. A. (2018). The Liber de existencia riveriarum (c.1200) and the Birth of Nautical Cartography. *Imago Mundi, 71*(1), 1–21. doi:10.1080/03085694.2019.1529898

Gössling, S., Hanna, P., Higham, J., Cohen, S., & Hopkins, D. (2019). Can we fly less? Evaluating the 'necessity' of air travel. *Journal of Air Transport Management, 81*. doi:10.1016/j.jairtraman.2019.101722

Healy, G., Laurie, N. and Hope, J. (2023). Creating stories of educational change in and for geography: what can we learn from Bolivia and Peru? *Geography. 108*(2), 64–73.

Hedding, D., & Breetzke, G. (2021). 'Here be dragons!' The gross under-representation of the Global South on editorial boards in Geography. *The Geographical Journal, 187*, 331–345. doi:10.1111/geoj.12405

Huaman, E. S. (2022). How indigenous scholarship changes the field: Pluriversal appreciation, decolonial aspirations, and comparative indigenous education. *Comparative Education Review, 66*(3), 391–416. doi:10.1086/720442

Ingold, T. (2016). *Lines*. Abingdon: Routledge.

Lewis, C. S. (1955). *Surprised by Joy: The Shape of My Early Life*. London: Geoffrey Bles.

Livingstone, D. N. (1992). *The Geographical Tradition: Episodes in the History of a Contested Enterprise*. Oxford: Blackwell.

Mabogunje, A. L. (2002). Poverty and environmental degradation: Challenges within the global economy. *Environment: Science and Policy for Sustainable Development, 44*(1), 8–19. doi:10.1080/00139150209605588

Mabogunje, A. L. (2004). Geography in the Nigerian public policy domain: The impact and influence of American geographers. *GeoJournal, 59*(1), 63–67.

Massey, D. (2005). *For Space*. London: Sage.

McKittrick, K. (2006). *Demonic Grounds: Black Women and the Cartographies of Struggle*. London: University of Minnesota Press.

McKittrick, K. (2021a). Dear April: The Aesthetics of Black Miscellanea. *Antipode, 54*(1), 3–18. doi:10.1111/anti.12773

McKittrick, K. (2021b). *Dear Science and Other Stories*. Durham: Duke University Press.

Müller, M. (2021). Worlding geography: From linguistic privilege to decolonial anywheres. *Progress in Human Geography, 45*(6), 1440–1466. doi:10.1177/0309132520979356

Oancea, A., & Bridges, D. (2009). Philosophy of education in the UK: The historical and contemporary tradition. *Oxford Review of Education, 35*(5), 553–553.

Radcliffe, S. A. (2017). Decolonising geographical knowledges. *Transactions of the Institute of British Geographers, 42*(3), 329–333. doi:10.1111/tran.12195

Telford, A., Valentine, A., & Godby, S. (2023). The paradox of the 'sustainable fieldtrip'? Exploring the links between geography fieldtrips and environmental sustainability. *Journal of Geography in Higher Education*, 1–18. doi:10.1080/03098265.2023.2190961

Walford, R. (2001). *Geography in British Schools, 1850–2000: Making a World of Difference*. London: Woburn.

Zhishan, Z. (1993). Columbus and China. *Monumenta Serica, 41*, 177–187.

7 What stories should we tell?

Introduction

> All we know about time and space, or rather history and geography, is more than anything else imaginative.
>
> (Said, 1978, p. 55)

> The story opens the door to curiosity; the reams of evidence dissipate as we tell the world differently, with a creative precision. The story asks that we live with the difficult and frustrating ways of knowing differentially.
>
> (McKittrick, 2021, p. 7)

This book's subtitle, *reclaiming exploration to inspire curriculum and pedagogy*, is fundamentally about reclaiming the stories we tell about the world and about geography. Exploration comes to be known through the stories that are told about it (Maslen, 2020), just as the world we know is itself constructed through interweaving, partial, contradictory narratives that are written and rewritten; blending accounts, counternarratives, evidence, theory, beliefs, feelings, policy and data. Asking *What stories should we tell*, this final chapter begins by arguing for the importance of story in teaching geography. So, my first response is to make explicit the assumption behind this question: a call to tell more stories, and to use ideas about narrative to shape curriculum and pedagogy more deeply.[1] Throughout this book, I have highlighted some of the stories that have been told about geography and about teaching geography. In particular, I have critiqued the kinds of environmental determinism and Empire-building geographies that have told racist stories about the world and its peoples. These stories build narratives about space-time, development, progress and cultures in ways that construct a hyper-real Europe in contrast to an ahistorical, uncivilised Africa/Other. The plot follows a linear path of progress in which the main characters revolve around heroic individual explorers bravely forging the path of civilisation and development. My critique of these stories involved questioning the narrative of the plot by pointing to the

 DOI: 10.4324/9781003321682-7

multiple ways in which the 'others' to which Europeans journeyed were in many ways highly sophisticated, cultured and wealthy. It also involved questioning the characters, unpicking the myth-making about lone individuals to instead appreciate the wide range of people on whom they relied: the production of 'Western' knowledge relied deeply and is hard to disentangle from Indigenous knowledge, information and expertise. These critiques give some negative pointers to the kinds of stories that we might want to rethink. Against these narrow stories that have constructed simplistic myths about nations, hierarchies and progress, I want to suggest some ways of telling more expansive and more generous stories that speak to the complexity and wonder of the world and its peoples: stories that invite young people into the geographical adventure to stimulate their own explorations of this incredible, bewildering, awe-inspiring, unequal, hopeful, violent, beautiful and, currently, rapidly warming world. I do this through three aspects of stories: locations; characters and plots, after a more general discussion of the idea of storytelling and using story in teaching.

Stories have been described as 'psychologically privileged'.[2] Story-driven experiences function at multiple levels, including perceptual and emotional. The perceptual level of experience is about the striking mental images that stories evoke. The clarity of these images creates experiences that are highly memorable. The emotional level is about our reactions that are driven by connections we recognise between the narrative's values and those of our – and our students' – own experiential background (Caracciolo, 2014). When we read or listen to stories, we are very likely to understand and be able to work out what's going on (including making inferences about how characters are feeling and so on that we are not explicitly told about), and we are also likely to remember the story at a later date. This remembering is often in quite impressive detail as we begin retelling, sparking connections between events, characters, locations and the unfolding narrative. In their meta-analysis of previous studies that had tested this idea (asking: *does story help with understanding and remembering?*), Mar et al. (2021) looked across 150 effect sizes, and across these studies together they had included over 33,000 participants. They contrast the understanding and remembering that comes through two different types of texts: narrative and expository. They describe narrative texts as mostly being found in novels or short stories. Aspects of the 'familiar structure' of the narrative includes a recognisable 'story grammar' including setting, theme, plot and resolution. In narrative, there is a focus on characters and their development, actions and the consequences of these actions. The headline conclusion across these studies is that 'people had an easier time comprehending and recalling narrative texts compared to expository ones' (p. 745). They summarise theoretical reasons for the effectiveness of narrative across a range of arguments (p. 733): stories are more familiar (from the youngest of ages, children are often told stories and through these experiences they become acquainted with the idea and format of a story in ways that they do not engage with expository texts until much later in life); stories often resemble and make connections with familiar everyday experiences; stories often engage our emotions; stories focus on social relationships, and the interpersonal relationships, friendships, arguments, and more are all themes and experiences that we are deeply familiar with; and our experiences of life as events that are temporally ordered relates strongly to the grammar of story. 'The close parallels between narratives and how we communicate our own experiences has led to stories being described as close to the "language of the mother tongue"' (p. 733). Against these markers of familiarity, they contrast the unfamiliar nature of expository texts (such as textbooks, manuals and curricula) and their main structure which 'often resembles a pyramid, with the theme introduced first (i.e. the tip of the pyramid) and this theme subsequently elaborated on at length' (p. 733). Familiarity with narrative is referred to in the cognitive science literature as being a part of students' prior knowledge. Being already equipped with this knowledge helps students to understand the information quicker, make inferences and draw more sophisticated connections within the particular issue they are currently working on, and more broadly across schemes of work, subjects, and whole phases of education.

Geography has always been about telling stories. The expeditions that I discussed above are known through the stories that have been told about them. 'Raw experience' is known, even for those experiencing it first-hand, through the lens of our stories about the world. I have made explicit some of the problematic ways in which these stories have been told, so hopefully it is clear that we need to change and expand the stories we tell. But the central idea – telling stories and using narrative – is essential, and doing this better holds significant promise for making geography a subject fit for the twenty-first century and beyond. Story should have an important place in teaching, and we might think of the use and value of story across scales; stories within individual explanations, single lessons, schemes of work, academic years and whole phases of education.

Big stories

In thinking about telling more stories in geography teaching, and before moving to use ideas about plot, characters and conflict, we might reflect further on, and critically examine, our own stories. Teachers are not disinterested, depersonalised deliverers of a curriculum, but are persons relating to other persons in classrooms and other settings. What it means to be a person is obviously an incredibly complex question (Nwoye, 2017; Smith, 2003), and one that is central to ideas about the aims and purposes of education. In the lecture *Educating Persons*, Richard Pring (2004) uses the idea of 'moral seriousness' to explore questions about education in the context of these amazing begins- humans! His summary of the essentially moral purpose of education is about:

> Helping each one to become more fully a person and to realize what is essentially human about themselves and others; the inseparable link between such personal development and membership of a community which respects

> each person; respect for the continuum of experiences between home and formal schooling; attaching central importance to social interaction between student and student, and student and teacher; drawing upon the intellectual resources of the academic disciplines (the public meanings); and recognition of each person's authentic response to those explorations.
>
> (p. 38)

What does it mean to become more fully human, and what role should education – and geography education in particular – play in this? How would you tell the story you have been a part of in relation to this? In the Nuffield-funded review of 14–19 Education and Training – *Education For All* – Pring and colleagues (2009) expressed this question as 'What counts as an educated 19 year old in this day and age?' I am raising these more fundamental questions here to connect them with our discussion of story and narrative. The critiques of accounts of school geography that I have offered in various places throughout this book have in part been driven by a dissatisfaction with these other stories about geography, but most importantly the critiques are driven by these more basic beliefs about equality of respect for persons, regardless of their socio-economic background, nationality, gender, race, ethnicity, class, or anything else. In thinking about the ways that we might use narrative in teaching, it is also vital to critically reflect on the kinds of stories that we see ourselves ('ourselves' in the biggest sense) as being a part of and contributing to, both in a descriptive sense (accurately describing what these stories are like) and normatively (as we work to bring into being what *should* be the case). Smith's (2010) account of this question *What is a Person?* emphasises the importance of story to how we make sense of the world and ourselves. He also addresses the argument that we no longer need to tell stories about the world and our place in it, partly in relation to a postmodern 'incredulity toward metanarratives' that is sometimes seen as a part of our apparent rejection or side-lining of the overarching stories that locate us:

> We moderns no longer have to huddle around fires telling fanciful myths about creations, floods, trials, conquests, and hoped-for paradises. Science, industry, rationality, and technology have dispelled the darkness and ignorance that once held the human race captive to its fanciful fables. Today, through progress, enlightenment, and cultural evolution, we now possess positive knowledge, scientific facts, rational analyses. We no longer need to be a people of ballads and legends, for we are a people of periodic tables, technical manuals, genetic maps and computer codes...We are now educated, rational, analytical. Indeed, by struggling to break out of the fear and ignorance of our ancestral myth-making past into the clear daylight of rational, scientific knowledge, we have opened up for the human race a future of greater prosperity, longevity, and happiness.
>
> (Smith, 2003, pp. 63–64)

Having briefly retold this modern story about progress and humanity, Smith argues that he is not saying this story is false, but rather that telling a story like this as a means of making sense of the world and our place in it continues to be vital for humans:

> For all of our science, rationality, and technology, we moderns are no less the makers, tellers, and believers of narrative construals of existence, history, and purpose than were our forebears at any other time in human history. But more than that, we not only continue to be animals who make stories but also animals who are made by our stories. We tell and retell narratives that themselves come fundamentally to constitute and direct our lives.
>
> (p. 64)

These big stories raise vital questions about our beliefs about persons, nations, progress, development and more. Some of the stories that are relevant to this discussion are very close to home, such as the stories we tell about the students we teach, and I want to suggest that we critically reflect here on the same questions about naming (think; bright, smart, naughty, lazy, thick, high ability, low ability…). There is an awesome responsibility on teachers both in terms of the knowledge, values and beliefs that students rely on their teachers for, and also on the kinds of beliefs (in the widest sense, the *naming*) that we do of students. What do we expect of them? What opportunities, freedoms and responsibilities do we create? One provocation from Biesta (2020) foregrounds ideas about risk and freedom for students to 'exist as subject':

> This partly is the 'big' question as to whether there is space for students to exist within educational situations and settings. But it is also a very practical question, in that in education we should make room for students' sense-making – which teachers indeed cannot do for their students – and for exploring the unknown and the not-yet-known. Even within the context of sound curriculum thinking, squeezing the risk out of education is simply uneducational. In this regard, risk is important and relevant for education's sake…
>
> (p. 103)

Reclaimed ideas about exploration to inspire geography teaching creates space for risk. What kinds of risks might we take with the plots through which we structure teaching?

Plots

Plots are central to the idea of storytelling, helping 'the story 'do' what it 'does' by showing the point of the story' (Paton & Kotzee, 2021, p. 430). The plot connects the otherwise disparate aspects of the narrative, bringing together 'different events and episodes into a meaningful whole' (Lawler, 2008, p. 35). Focusing on this aspect of story, we might ask: what is the plot that ties the lesson together? How might the otherwise potentially disparate elements be more strongly and memorably tied together through a clearer plot? And beyond having a plot and making this a clearer part of our teaching, what kinds of plots might we create? In the context of this particular book about adventure in geography teaching and *reclaiming* exploration, I also want to highlight the ways in which we might reclaim and rethink the kinds of plots that we use to tell stories about geography and about the world. Some of these plots are about the big stories we tell about nations, progress and development; questions that I have opened in various ways through the chapters above. Yusoff's (2018) reshaping and retelling of the plot line of geology in *A Billion Black Anthropocenes or None* offers a critical example of the way that even a single word – in that case, Anthropocene – comes packaged with a plot line that already positions people in certain ways and smuggles in assumptions about responsibility. This unpicking of a single word is a brilliant example of the connotations and values that come with the terms we use; of the stories they are already attached to and continue to tell. The history of geography means that many of these stories carry deep striations of Empire. In response to the shape of these plotlines, in Esson and Last's (2020) terms, attention to race and racism need to be foregrounded to build anti-racist practices in geography teaching. They ask:

> [H]ow do we address the racial coding of Geography curricula so that we question more directly the validity of our present order of geographical knowledge itself? One way to undertake this creative experimentation is by looking at what happens when we attend to race and racism within the narratives around the histories we construct about the geographical tools we use, including the compass, maps (e.g., the Tabula Rogeriana), and calculations.
>
> (Esson & Last, 2020, p. 672)

Following their prompt, this vision for reclaiming exploration in teaching geography does not mean rejecting all of the previous work in the field and replacing it with something else. Instead, the popular tales are unpicked and expanded. Or to use Chakrabarty's (2000) expression, the popular dominant accounts are 'provincialized': they are turned from generalised master stories to more complex co-accounts.

> As should be clear by now, provincializing Europe is not a project of rejecting or discarding European thought. Relating to a body of thought to which one largely owes one's intellectual existence cannot be a matter of exacting what Leela Gandhi has aptly called "postcolonial revenge." European thought is at once both indispensable and inadequate in helping us to think through the experiences of political modernity in non-Western nations, and

> provincializing Europe becomes the task of exploring how this thought – which is now everybody's heritage and which affect us all – may be renewed from and for the margins.
>
> (p. 16)

Renewing from and for the margins echoes the discussion in Chapter 6 about re-thinking where we should start from. It also adds this question about where our teaching is for. Who benefits? Where benefits? Who benefits from the plot being structured in this particular way?

Before moving to discuss characters, I want to highlight the ways in which the idea of plots might be particularly useful for engaging with data and statistics in geography teaching. I introduced some of these ideas through Blastland and Dilnot's review of BBC impartiality, and their wider body of work questioning the ways in which the media and politicians use and abuse statistics. Much of this misuse is about the stories that they want to tell through statistics, because the media and the politicians know that it is the story constructed around the statistic that carries the power. The plot lines in which data and statistics are presented and help to construct are important to critically consider. From the perspective of teaching about research methods, there is also potential to make greater use of narrative as statistical tests are introduced to students. Research in mathematics education suggests that making greater use of students' own contextualised stories might help them to make sense of statistics. For example, Sherwood and Makar's (2022) study *Students making sense of statistics through storytelling* suggests that presenting the content in relation to narrative, and also engaging students with a dialogue between the subject matter and their own narratives, helped to address the challenges often presented by fear (of statistics and mathematics more broadly) and highly abstract material. Interestingly, they also found that students don't naturally make connections between the statistics and their own stories. Yet 'once they did so, their stories helped initiate pathways of success for making sense of their statistical learning' (p. 2). There is scope to apply this idea across topics that students feel intimidated or challenged by; engaging with narrative and making meaningful connections to the plot lines that they are a part of: plots that provide the framework for the story to come alive as characters interact.

Characters

Characters are normally people, sometimes animals, and in the context of geography teaching might also be places, theories and models. Things with agency that are acting on the world. Re-thinking them as characters might only involve a subtle tweak but has the potential to open a more creative and richer engagement. So, an early question to ask is, for any given activity, lesson, or scheme of work: who are the main characters? In this discussion, I focus on ideas about characters in relation to theory, representation, naming and nature.

Theories and models are too often presented without narrative, bursting onto the scene with little background or history. They are the main focus of Mar's expository texts discussed above. We might be so keen to accurately communicate the central features of the model, and to ensure that students have precise definitions and clear understandings (all good things!), that the broader context – which comes wrapped up with various kinds of messiness and uncertainty – might be given less attention. Where did they come from? Who produced them? When? In what context and in response to what kinds of debates and to address what issues or questions? Through what processes did they make their journeys into the classroom? What effects do they have on the world? Here, there is interesting scope to play with the ways that theory and models – as characters in the narrative – might be rethought to deepen our critical understanding and engagement with them as they act in and on the world. Deepening our understanding of theory and models also speaks to a richer conception of the ways that they function. McKittrick describes how she

> understands theory as a form of storytelling. Stories and storytelling signal the fictive work of theory. I hope this move, momentarily, exposes the intricacies of academic work where fact-finding, experimentation, analysis, study are recognized as narrative, plot, tale and incomplete inventions, rather than impartial treatises.
>
> (McKittrick, 2021, pp. 7–8)

Asking what characters – *who* – features in our stories can be revolutionary and have huge implications for what the story looks like (Dodds Pennock, 2022). In particular:

> Too often the history of peoples of colour in Europe is marginalised or deliberately suppressed, their presence in the past ignored. Too often their contribution to the contemporary world is a footnote or a sidebar, and interesting anecdote or a local-interest story. But Indigenous people were, and are, and should be, central characters in this history.
>
> (p. 243)

More than merely being included, *how* characters are represented is also important. In asking the question *Should we only teach about real people and places?* (Puttick, 2017), I drew attention to the use of 'talking heads' in textbooks and geography teaching resources. Photographs of un-named people with speech bubbles imposed on them with views of the typical farmer/local and so on. Ethical questions about attribution and use of images and perspectives are rarely made explicit in these resources. Who are these people? What do they think about the viewpoint attributed to them? What about their 'look' means that they were seen as appropriate for being used as a representative of this perspective? What are the patterns in our choices about what certain groups or viewpoints 'look like'? What unwritten assumptions about the world are we communicating to students? I gave some stark examples of the whiteness of representation in Walford's *Geography in British Schools* in Chapter 3, and the stark contrast between the representation of white characters with the exception of the 'almost unclad Aboriginal'. In Chakrabarty's (2000, p. 94) terms, 'the figure of the subaltern is necessarily mediated by problems of representation'.

The un-named talking heads are potentially problematic in part because of the un-addressed ethical questions about their own views about the viewpoints attributed to them. Questions about representation are also more obviously related to the names that we use to refer to people and places. In her book *On Savage Shores: How Indigenous Americans Discovered Europe*, Dodds Pennock (2022) outlines the traumatic history of settler colonialism in North America,[3] beginning with questions about the names we use to refer to peoples. These names matter because of what they say 'about who we are, who we were, and how others see our relationship to them. For Indigenous peoples, who have been historically oppressed, marginalised and insulted, names matter even more' (p.xiiv). Her approach towards deciding what terms to use to refer to different peoples seems to be a good principle to apply to decisions in geography teaching about the names we choose to use: to 'respect tribal, national and individual identities by calling people by the names they called themselves' (p.xvi). This completely inverts the approach of Da Gama and others of immediately imposing new names on places and peoples.

Questions about what names to use demand attention and sensitivity to detail; to the importance, significance and value of each word that we use. In his ode to Barry Lopez (author of, among many other things, the masterpiece *Arctic Dreams: Imagination and Desire in a Northern Landscape*), Robert Macfarlane describes the 'keynote – a grace note, really' of Lopez's work as the importance of speaking 'with precisions about the places you inhabit and that inhabit you':

> to sharpen perception—and to begin to honor the immense complexities, human and more-than-human, of a given landscape and its communities. Good place-language, well used, opens onto mystery, grows knowledge, and summons wonder. And in the absence of an exact and detail-giving lexis, the living world can blur into a generalized wash of green, becoming an easily disposable backdrop.[4]

Macfarlane's own body of work provides many inspiring examples opening onto mystery, growing knowledge and summoning wonder. His collaboration with the artist Jackie Morris, *The Lost Words*, speaks to this need to retain the wonder of this place-language through which we might better understand and appreciate the living world. They both signed an open letter[5] calling for words removed from the Oxford University Press' Junior Dictionary to be returned. Such words include; acorn, bluebell, conker, heron and kingfisher. *The Lost Words* is full of 'spells' and artwork intended to be read aloud, pondered over, to bring the words – and the flora and fauna they point to – alive, to be known, noticed and connected with: nature as 'alive, powerful and sentient', rather than something that can merely be 'watched, consumed, ignored'.[6]

Conflict

The film opens with the image of a body floating on the Mediterranean Sea, 60 miles south of Marseilles. There is a light flashing on the body. The body looks limp, lifeless. The title THE BOURNE IDENTITY flashes across the screen before passing fishermen pull the body out of the water. "You've never seen a dead body before?" says one fisherman to another. Immediately, questions come into the viewer's mind: Who is this man? Why is his body in the middle of the Mediterranean? Why is there a light strapped to him? It is not long before one of his rescuers is investigating and pulling out bullets from his back. Why has he been shot? Who did it? Shortly after, he comes awake and has his own questions: Initially *what the hell are you doing to me?!* then 'What is my name? Where am I? Why do I have the account details to a bank in Zurick on some crazy LED thing in my back?!' The ensuing trilogy sets about discovering the answers to this dilemma. We the viewers are drawn into this conflict – into this 'point of tension' – and we *need* to find out who he was, where he came from, why people are trying to kill him. And so we watch, engaging with his story.

To give another example: on a road in Kenya an old land rover falls over onto its side, and with a bang, flocks of flamingos fly into the air. Another car full of men with guns and radios immediately arrives, removes one of the bodies, dumps it in the back of their own truck and drives away. In another place, a man has just said goodbye to his wife, who has then walked across an airstrip with a different man. As they near the plane the picture blurs to white. They are due back two days later. We soon discover that two days later a woman and her driver were then found dead. They had stayed in a hotel together. In one room. Who are they? Was she having an affair? Who killed them? Why? Was it planned? Again, the whole story has been set up: the foundations are laid and our minds are grappling with a host of issues: the point of tension that needs to be resolved. We have generated questions that need answers, being drawn into the stories of these people that we now want to understand.

How might lessons begin by establishing a point of tension that engages students, capturing them to such a degree that they *need* to solve the problem and discover the answers? Interestingly, while trends in classroom lessons have been to make the 'learning objectives' explicit (often as a statement copied from the board at the start of the lesson), or for students to complete a recall activity (such as a short quiz to test their memory on terms and definitions previously learnt) none of these films communicate the point of tension explicitly. Instead, the opening scenes work successfully to provoke the same questions that need to be resolved in all our minds. They force *us* to think up the equivalent of the learning objectives, and rather than being given these objectives, we actively create them ourselves and on our own terms: we work out what we are keen to discover and get involved in the adventure.

Some tensions might be resolved in a single lesson, whereas others might endure across whole schemes of work and longer. The complexity and depth of some of the questions with which geographers are wrestling – and the partiality of our understandings – means that keeping hold of some sense of openness and incompleteness is vital. These questions are not simple, neither are they solved. Humanity does not have the answers yet. Some of the global challenges I mentioned, such as climatic and environmental crises, are urgent ongoing questions: how should we live? What part can geography play in understanding and responding to these challenges? Maybe the ongoing narrative conflict of colonialism: striations of Empire in school geography that I have been exposing and critiquing throughout the book are at the heart of conflicts that need to be solved. There are striations of Empire in school geography that continue to demand reparations, and given the historic foundation of today's inequalities, how should geography respond? In Pete's (2018) terms: 'I want my non-Indigenous colleagues to take greater responsibility for exposing settler-colonialism because it is – ultimately – their story' (p. 180). How can we tell better stories about the world and about geography itself? Or to frame this in another way, moving beyond Conrad's epochs of Geography Fabulous, Geography Militant and Geography Triumphant, by what kinds of geographies do we want our work to be known, and the students of geography in today's schools to be developing? Geographies *Just*? Sustainable? Geography Generous?[7] The way that we use conflict, and the terms that we use through this to represent people, places, theories, models and more are important, and hopefully this discussion about narrative is an encouragement to take particular care with how we name and frame things and relations. To revisit Macfarlane's point, 'define' isn't quite the right term for this kind of careful use; *evoke* might be closer to our hopes for our use of these words.

Here's to the storytellers

Through out this book, I have tried to critically examine some of the dominant stories that have been told about geography and about the world under the (probably overly ambitious) aim of *reclaiming exploration to inspire curriculum and pedagogy*. Concluding this chapter with the subtitle 'here's to the storytellers', I have two groups of storytellers in mind. You, readers and teachers of geography, and those geographers whose work ours relies on and engages with. To begin with the latter, at the end of the brilliant *Dear Science,* McKittrick does not call her reference list References or Bibliography. Instead, the title she gives the list is Storytellers. Questions about whom we engage with and cite have run throughout our discussions. I have critiqued the Anglo-American dominance of the subject and have joined calls for expanding and Worlding this subject that claims and desires to understand more about the world. In pointing to the politics of citation, and foregrounding questions about where we start from, the contingencies and incompleteness of my own reading and references will be obvious. There are silences and exclusions; people and places not represented here, and those whose names and work are not honoured here for a variety of reasons, mostly related to my own limitations, of which the most immediate is that I can only read academic articles in English. But, accepting all of that, I hope this book is an encouragement for school geography to engage more explicitly and more expansively with the incredible range and diversity of storytellers who are doing geography.

The striations of Empire in school geography run deep, and I hope that teachers who engage with this book might be able to more readily recognise and unpick some of these enduring legacies. Where geography's imperial past used geographical tools for domination and control, my hope through this book has been to reclaim exploration to nurture wonder and tell better stories that work towards more just, equitable and sustainable futures. In the context of European anthropology museums, Hicks (2020) describes the challenge as being an urgent twin task of using their

> status as unique public spaces and indexes of enduring colonial histories to change the stories we tell ourselves about the British Empire, while taking action in support of communities across the Global South in building museums on a totally new kind of model.
>
> (p. 35)

So too for school geography, Hicks' twin task might be a useful way of thinking about reclaiming exploration to inspire in a deep and holistic sense: What kinds of new models of geography education might support greater equality globally? How might we use geography education and its status and potential to change the stories we tell ourselves about the world and about geography itself? Adventure lies ahead, as yet unwritten. Invite your students to explore it and help to write this next chapter in the story of human drama being played out in the Anthropocene. Inspire them to learn from mistakes the subject has produced so that together they can tell better stories.

Once upon a time, geographers…

Questions and activities

How has this book challenged your understandings of geography and exploration?

In what ways does school geography perpetuate the Striations of Empire? How might these striations be addressed, at individual, departmental, school, local, regional, national and global levels?

What is the significance of storytelling in geography education? What are the benefits of using storytelling in geography education for understanding, remembering, engaging and inspiring? What challenges and limitations can you see with using storytelling and narrative in geography education?

What examples do you have of stories that have been told about and through geography that perpetuate inequality across multiple dimensions?

What examples do you have, and can you create, that invite young people into the geographical adventure and stimulate their own (*reclaimed*) explorations of the world?

How can we use narrative principles and tools to teach about geography and the world in more expansive and more generous ways?

What new models of geography education might support greater equality globally?

Ask students to read about and research a geographer or a group of geographers whose work is often excluded or marginalised in Anglo-American stories about geography. What can we learn from their perspectives? What do they reveal previous 'blindness' to?

Encourage students to critically examine geography textbooks and identify Striations of Empire and omissions in the stories that are told about geography and about the world.

Starting with a single lesson or a single activity, plan how to make greater use of storytelling and narrative tools to enhance teaching and learning.

How can re-thinking theoretical concepts and models *as characters* in narrative help students to deepen their critical understanding of them? Research the creation and history of a theoretical concept or model and then present it as a character in a narrative, for example, including details such as who produced there where in what context and through what process has it changed.

What are some of the ethical questions surrounding the use of images of un-named talking heads in geography teaching resources? How might the representation of characters in geography teaching resources impact students' understandings of the world and their perspectives? What are the implications of using respectful and accurate names for people and places in geography teaching? How can speaking with greater precision about the places we inhabit help to deepen our understanding and appreciation of them?

How might we use geography education to tell better stories about the world that inspire more just equitable and sustainable futures? What new stories might you tell?

Notes

1 While there is no space here to expand the discussion of making greater use of storytelling beyond ITE and teachers' ongoing CPD, Paton and Kotzee's (2021) discussion of storytelling and practical wisdom in the ethics education of junior doctors offers one example of its generative potential in a range of different situations.

2 For example, see: https://kbsgk12project.kbs.msu.edu/wp-content/uploads/2011/02/Ask-the-Cognitive-Scientist.pdf
3 See Dodds Pennock (2022), Kimmerer (2020) and Pete (2018, p. 179), on referring to North America as Turtle Island https://www.aaihs.org/rethinking-black-life-on-turtle-island/ and https://www.un.org/en/academic-impact/keeping-turtle-island-alive-—mohawk's-fight-against-industrial-pollution. Replacing and reclaiming commonly accepted names for places can be a helpful provocation to help spark realisation that such names are neither 'natural' nor obvious.
4 https://orionmagazine.org/article/barry-lopez-from-here-to-the-horizon/
5 http://www.naturemusicpoetry.com/uploads/2/9/3/8/29384149/letter_to_oup_final.pdf
6 https://www.theguardian.com/books/2017/sep/30/robert-macfarlane-lost-words-children-nature The John Muir trust have also made some accompanying teaching ideas available on their website: https://www.johnmuirtrust.org/assets/000/002/735/PSM_Workshop_Report_2023_original.pdf?1677252476
7 https://orionmagazine.org/article/barry-lopez-from-here-to-the-horizon/

References

Biesta, G. (2020). Risking ourselves in education: Qualification, socialization, and subjectification revisited. *Educational Theory, 70*(1), 89–104.

Caracciolo, M. (2014). *The Experiantiality of Narrative: An Enactivist Approach*. Berlin: De Gruyter.

Chakrabarty, D. (2000). *Provincializing Europe*. Oxford: Princeton University Press.

Dodds Pennock, C. (2022). *On Savage Shores: How Indigenous Americans Discovered Europe*. London: Weidenfeld & Nicolson.

Esson, J., & Last, A. (2020). Anti-racist learning and teaching in British geography. *Area*, area.12658-area.12658. doi:10.1111/area.12658

Hicks, D. (2020). *The Brutish Museums: The Benin Bronzes, Colonial Violence and Cultural Restitution*. London: Pluto Press.

Kimmerer, R. W. (2020). *Braiding Sweetgrass: Indigenous Wisdom, Scientific Knowledge and the Teachings of Plants*. London: Penguin.

Lawler, S. (2008). Stories and the social world. In M. Pickering (Ed.), *Research Methods for Cultural Studies* (pp. 32–49). Edinburgh: Edinburgh University Press.

Mar, R. A., Li, J., Nguyen, A. T. P., & Ta, C. P. (2021). Memory and comprehension of narrative versus expository texts: A meta-analysis. *Psychonomic Bulletin & Review, 28*(3), 732–749. doi:10.3758/s13423-020-01853-1

Maslen, S. (2020). Between narrative and practice: Storytelling as a way of knowing how to be in nature. *Ethnography, 23*(4), 433–449. doi:10.1177/1466138120923707

McKittrick, K. (2021). *Dear Science and Other Stories*. Durham: Duke University Press.

Nwoye, A. (2017). An Africentric theory of human personhood. *Psychology in Society, 54*, 42–66. doi:10.17159/2309-8708/2017/n54a4

Paton, A., & Kotzee, B. (2021). The fundamental role of storytelling and practical wisdom in facilitating the ethics education of junior doctors. *Health, 25*(4), 417–433. doi:10.1177/1363459319889102

Pete, S. (2018). Meschachakanis, a coyote narrative: Decolonising higher education. In G. K. Bhambra, K. Nisancioglu, & D. Gebrial (Eds.), *Decolonising the University* (pp. 173–189). London: Pluto Press.

Pring, R. (2004). *Philosophy of Education: Aims, Theory, Common Sense and Research*. London: Continuum.

Pring, R., Hayward, G., Hodgson, A., Johnson, J., Kepp, E., Oancea, A., ... Wilde, S. (2009). *Education for All. The Future of Education and Training for 14–19 Year Olds*. London: Routledge.

Puttick, S. (2017). Should we only teach about real people and real places? *Geography, 102*(1), 26–32.

Said, E. (1978). *Orientalism*. London: Penguin.

Sherwood, C., & Makar, K. (2022). Students making sense of statistics through storytelling: A theoretical perspective based on Bruner's narrative mode of thought. *Mathematics Education Research Journal*. doi:10.1007/s13394-022-00440-y

Smith, C. (2003). *Moral, Believing Animals: Human Personhood and Culture*. Oxford: Oxford University Press.

Smith, C. (2010). *What Is a Person? Rethinking Humanity, Social Life, and the Moral Good from the Person Up*. London: University of Chicago Press.

Yusoff, K. (2018). *A Billion Black Anthropocenes or None*. Minneapolis: University of Minnesota Press.

Index

abstraction 45, 58
adventure 1–4, 6–10, 13–15, 18–19, 22, 24, 27, 35, 54, 56, 74, 76–77, 87, 92, 99–100, 103, 115, 119, 124–126
Africa 14, 19–23, 28, 38, 39–40, 42–43, 45, 64–65, 67–69, 72, 75, 77, 81, 93, 95, 97–98, 114
agency 7, 45, 64, 89, 120
Anglo-American 82, 84, 88, 92, 124, 126; see also Euro-American
Asia 38–40, 72, 75–77, 97, 110
Australia 19, 33, 36, 38, 42, 80

Black 3, 20–22, 33–34, 38, 45–46, 53–54, 65, 89, 109, 119
blind 22–23, 26, 27, 65, 83

Calicut 15–16
Chakrabarty, D. 3, 13, 23, 37, 40, 58, 69, 119, 122
characters 53, 89, 93, 114–116, 120–122
children 1, 4, 5, 9, 25, 36, 82, 115; see also students
Christian 15, 18, 24, 43, 47, 58
city 5–6, 15, 19, 58, 59, 74, 108, 111
classroom 8–9, 33, 54–55, 58, 71, 88, 92, 103, 121, 123
climate 2, 6, 24, 59, 82, 109; change 4, 5, 11, 59, 60, 79, 80, 81, 82, 83, 85, 87, 88, 108
cluster concept 54–55
colonial 1–2, 9, 13–15, 27, 29, 30–33, 35–37, 40–44, 47–50, 53–56, 65, 67–68, 70–71, 78–79, 89, 95, 101, 125
coloniality 66, 99
colonialism 20, 24, 29, 30, 37, 40–41, 43–44, 50, 68, 108, 110, 122, 124
conceptual 6, 54, 55, 57, 60, 62
conflict 9, 108, 116, 123–124
Congo 19–23
critical 1–2, 13, 22, 26, 31, 33, 36, 40, 42, 50, 54, 69, 83–84, 87–89, 100, 110, 119, 121, 126
critically 3, 7, 9, 13–14, 27, 31, 43, 47, 50, 53, 71, 83–85, 93, 97, 116–118, 120, 124, 126
culture 5, 10, 28, 30, 41, 43, 45, 63, 65, 69–70, 76, 85, 109, 114–115
curriculum 2–3, 20, 31–32, 38, 55, 57, 59, 68, 94, 114, 116, 118, 124

Dawn Gill 35, 48, 51
Dear Science and Other Stories 3, 124
decolonial 8, 22, 35, 47, 53–54, 84, 93, 100
decolonising 54, 71
determinism 24, 34–36, 45–46, 57, 63–64, 71, 92, 95, 114
development 4, 24, 28, 38, 54, 55, 57, 62, 69, 70, 79, 80, 89, 98–99, 111, 114–116, 118–119
disciplinary 4, 7, 13, 54–55, 60, 62–63, 71

discipline 4, 7, 24, 26–27, 30–31, 34, 40, 55–56, 58, 70–71, 74, 84, 88, 92, 93, 98, 109, 117

embodied 5–6, 77
Empire 1–2, 9, 13–14, 20–22, 24, 26, 29–31, 34–36, 39, 40, 42–47, 49–51, 53, 56, 63, 70, 76, 77, 79, 94, 95, 114, 119, 124–126
England 19, 25, 30–31, 34, 36, 54, 66–67, 69, 79, 95, 97
environment 5–6, 36, 45, 50, 63, 67, 78, 87, 90
environmental 24, 34–35, 44, 64, 71, 92, 95, 108, 114, 124
epistemological 53, 63; see also knowledge
equitable 2, 71, 125–126
Euro-American 83, 93, 98, 109, 111; see also Anglo-American
Eurocentric 27, 40, 69, 98–99
Eurocentrism 1, 39, 40, 48, 110
Europe 3, 13, 14, 16, 21–23, 37, 38, 40, 65–66, 68, 69, 72, 75–77, 79–80, 89, 93–95, 98–99, 114, 119–122
European 7, 13–14, 16, 18–19, 21–23, 27, 37, 39–40, 42–43, 62, 66, 70, 75, 78, 79, 94–95, 98, 115, 119, 125
evidence 1, 7, 29–30, 35, 40, 43, 50, 83, 85, 99, 114
everyday 1, 3–4, 6–8, 10, 56–58, 61, 78, 84, 88–89, 92–93, 99–103, 108, 109, 110, 111, 115; see also local
expansive 2–3, 7, 84, 109, 115, 126
experience 3–4, 6, 10, 17–18, 21, 26–27, 32–33, 39–40, 45, 56–59, 61, 77, 95, 97, 99–101, 109, 115–117, 119
explore 3, 31, 49, 77, 79, 85, 95, 100, 111, 116, 125
explorer 1, 4, 17, 20, 26, 33, 35, 42, 75, 78–79, 92, 94, 97, 114
exploration 2–4, 6, 9, 13–14, 18–23, 25–27, 30, 34, 40, 42, 56, 61, 70, 77, 83, 84, 92–94, 98–101, 103, 108–109, 114–115, 117–119, 124–126
extraction 14, 19, 21, 23, 27, 44, 68, 70, 110
extractive 1, 4, 9, 26, 55, 56, 71, 76, 108

fieldwork 108–109, 112

Geographical Association 30, 85
Geography for the Young School Leaver 48–49
Global South 93, 98, 125
Gujarati 17, 18, 75, 95

humanity 2, 21–22, 27, 33, 37, 118, 124
hyper-real 23, 69, 75, 114

imperial 14, 20–21, 25, 29, 31, 34, 46, 76, 77, 79, 125
imperialism 2, 20–21, 22, 24, 27, 29, 40, 44, 50, 51
India 14–18, 25, 28, 37, 42–43, 77, 79, 81, 83, 95, 97, 111
indigenous 18, 28, 60, 65–67, 71, 78, 89, 93, 97, 99–100, 109, 121–122, 124
initial teacher education 4, 7, 54
information 1–2, 5, 9, 14–15, 18, 26, 45, 64, 74–76, 79–90, 92, 94, 97, 99, 101, 109, 112, 115–116
IPCC 59–60, 71

journey 2, 5, 14–19, 21, 24, 26, 50, 57, 68, 74–79, 83–84, 86–88, 92, 97, 108, 121
Joseph Conrad 2–3, 10, 19–23, 26–27, 124

Kolkata 15, 100–101, 109
knowledge 1, 3–11, 13–14, 17–18, 20–21, 25–26, 29–30, 32, 38–40, 45, 50, 53–62, 69–71, 74–79, 82–84, 88–89, 92, 94–95, 97–98, 100, 104, 109, 115–119, 122

learning 5, 7, 32, 56, 101, 103, 120, 123, 126
local 1, 3, 15, 26, 40, 50, 75–76, 78–79, 82, 84, 88, 92–93, 99, 100–101, 103, 108, 109, 110–112, 121, 125; see also everyday
London 6, 10, 28, 36, 48, 58, 64, 66, 99

Marco Polo 22–23, 27, 94
Mackinder, H. 33–37, 39, 41, 45, 49, 63, 67

McKittrick, K. 7, 38, 53, 93–94, 109, 111, 114, 121, 124
Marshall, T. 63, 65–69
majority 37, 47, 80, 99
map 2, 15, 19–20, 25, 38, 42, 50, 56, 64, 88, 94–98, 101, 107, 111, 117, 119
mapping 24, 57, 63, 106
Medieval 95, 97
minority 37, 66, 87, 94
mountain 37, 62–64, 76–78, 89
Muhammad al-Idrisi 95–97
Muslim 15, 18, 25
myth 13–14, 16–17, 24, 26, 28, 66, 69, 75, 79, 95, 97, 109, 115, 117

narrative 13, 17, 20, 23, 26–27, 32, 33, 40, 42, 68–69, 89, 93, 98, 109, 114–121, 124, 125–126, 128; see also story
National Geographic 19, 68

Ofsted 34, 36, 39, 49
orientalism 3, 92, 110
origin 13–14, 16–17, 20, 27, 39, 46, 64, 69, 79, 98
Oxford 7, 32–33, 45, 76, 81, 83, 88, 100, 103–106, 108, 109, 112, 122

pedagogical 7–9, 33, 55
pedagogy 2–3, 9, 39, 114, 124
PGCE 31–32
photograph 32–33, 96, 101, 103, 105–106, 108, 110, 121
political 7–9, 31, 34, 39, 48, 53, 66, 70, 76, 78, 85–86, 112, 119
plot 94, 114–116, 118–121
postcolonial 3, 8, 19, 29, 58, 62, 67, 93, 119
postcolonialism 29–30
power 1, 13, 29–30, 35, 50, 53, 55, 61, 66–67, 70, 84, 97, 120
powerful knowledge 1, 3, 10, 50, 53–62, 70–71, 74, 78
practical theorising 1, 6–9, 94, 97
Prisoners of Geography 1, 50, 53, 62–67, 69–71, 74–75
Provincializing Europe 3, 37, 119–120

race 14, 24, 32, 36, 38–39, 44, 47, 50–51, 53–54, 65–68, 98, 117, 119
racism 21, 33, 40–41, 45, 48–49, 54, 63–65, 69, 119
racist 1–2, 21, 22, 24, 26, 34–35, 39, 41–47, 49, 50, 53–54, 63, 114, 119
radical 9, 20, 47–50
reclaiming 2–4, 9, 42, 61, 92, 99, 108, 114, 119, 124–125, 127
Rhodes 44–45
Royal Geographical Society 21, 24–25, 30

school 1–4, 7, 10, 20, 24, 26, 29–35, 39–44, 46–51, 53–55, 57–59, 64, 71, 74–75, 79, 83, 86, 88, 92–93, 95, 100, 108, 117, 122, 124, 125
silence 53–54, 125
social 8, 32, 43, 47, 55, 66, 76, 85, 87–88, 112, 116–117
spatial 5, 30, 57, 60, 77, 78, 80, 112
statistics 83, 85–86, 120
stories 1–5, 9, 13–19, 22, 26–27, 31, 35, 40, 49, 51, 53, 63, 69, 70–71, 75, 78–79, 81, 85, 87–89, 92–95, 97–104, 106, 109, 111, 114–126
storytelling 89, 95, 115, 118, 120–121, 125–126; see also narrative
striations 1–2, 9, 24, 29–30, 32, 35, 39, 41, 43, 49–50, 53, 56, 119, 124–126
students 2, 4–5, 8–10, 30, 32–33, 50, 55–57, 62, 70–71, 74–75, 79, 87–88, 92, 94, 101, 103, 108–109, 111, 115–116, 118, 120–126; see also children
sustainable 2, 99, 112, 124–126

Tariq Jazeel 8, 10, 29–30, 50, 53, 58
teachers 1, 4–8, 14, 30–33, 36, 40–41, 44, 46, 48–49, 56, 61–62, 71, 74–75, 79–83, 85, 87–88, 101, 116, 118, 124–126
teaching 1–4, 6–10, 14, 24, 27, 30, 32, 35, 41, 48, 50, 54, 83–88, 92, 94, 99–100, 109–111, 115–122, 126–127
theory 7–8, 17, 35, 97, 114, 120–121

theoretical 26, 30, 40, 93, 97, 115, 126
time-space 63, 94–96

Vasco Da Gama 14–18, 26, 35, 68, 75, 79, 94–95, 111, 122
violence 19, 41, 44, 48, 64–65, 69, 89

Walford, R. 1, 30–36, 38–50, 53, 94–95, 99–100, 122
warfare 15, 23–24, 15
whiteness 32, 54, 66, 122
worlding 84, 88, 92, 98–99, 124
wonder 1–4, 9–10, 38, 63, 84, 100–101, 104, 115, 122, 125